U.S. Ratification of the
Human Rights Treaties

With or Without Reservations?

U.S. Ratification of the

Human Rights

Treaties

With or Without Reservations?

★

Edited for the
International Human Rights
Law Group
by
RICHARD B. LILLICH

UNIVERSITY PRESS OF VIRGINIA

Charlottesville

THE UNIVERSITY PRESS OF VIRGINIA
Copyright © 1981 by the Procedural Aspects of
International Law Institute, Inc.
200 Park Avenue, New York, New York 10017
First published 1981
ISBN 0–8139–0881–7

Library of Congress Cataloging in Publication Data
Main entry under title:

U. S. ratification of the human rights treaties with
or without reservations?

  Bibliography: p.
  1. Civil rights (International law)—Congresses. 2. Civil rights—United
States—Congresses. I. Lillich, Richard B. II. International Human Rights
Law Group, Washington, D.C.
K3239.6.U53   341.4′81   80–28995
ISBN 0–8139–0881–7

This volume may be cited as
U.S. RATIFICATION OF THE HUMAN RIGHTS TREATIES
WITH OR WITHOUT RESERVATIONS? (R. Lillich ed. 1981).
Printed in the United States of America

CONTENTS

*   *   *

PREFACE

*   *   *

In 1978 the Procedural Aspects of International Law Institute, with funding from the Ford Foundation and the Rockefeller Brothers Fund, established the International Human Rights Law Group in Washington, D.C. The Law Group, a nonprofit organization, provides legal services to individuals and nongovermental organizations on a *pro bono* basis. In an effort to educate the Bar and the general public about the importance and relevance of international human rights law, the Law Group sponsors a series of teaching seminars and occasional conferences on topics of current interest.

As part of this educational program the Law Group, on January 18, 1979, held a major conference on the ratification of the four human rights treaties that President Carter had transmitted to the Senate for its advice and consent on February 23, 1978. Until the President took this initiative, there had seemed little likelihood that the U.S. would become a party to these conventions, and for that reason relatively little attention had been paid to the constitutional aspects of U.S. ratification, much less to strategies by which such ratification might be achieved.

The President's message, while a step in the right direction, came as a distinct disappointment to most supporters of the conventions, since he recommended their ratification only with the addition of several dozen reservations, declarations, understandings, and statements, the most troublesome of which (at least for this writer) are the four declarations—one for each convention—which purport to make them non-self-executing and hence unenforceable in U.S. courts. Thus, while the President's general approach received considerable support, his overly cautious attitude toward ratification failed to stimulate the international law community to work for the conventions' ratification.

Accordingly, the Law Group organized the above-mentioned conference, designed to bring the leading international law experts on these conventions together to discuss the President's Message before an invited audience of nearly 100 nongovernmental organization representatives, government personnel (from both the Congress and the Executive), and other persons in a position to influence informed public opinion. The speakers' papers and edited remarks, together with a record of the discussion period, a reprint of the President's Message (which includes the text of the four conventions) and a selected bibliography of post-Message publications, make up this book.

Since the conference took place, the Senate Foreign Relations Committee has held four days of exploratory hearings on the conventions, but it has issued no report thereon and is expected to take no further action on them during 1980. Hence, the issues and alternatives raised and explored in this book remain of great topical interest. They are offered to the reader in the hope that he or she not only will perceive the importance of U.S. ratification of all four treaties but also will be moved to support and work actively for their adoption during the course of what undoubtedly will be a long ratification process.

Richard B. Lillich

Charlottesville, Virginia

U.S. Ratification of the
Human Rights Treaties

With or Without Reservations?

NIGEL RODLEY

* * *

On the Necessity of
United States Ratification
of the International
Human Rights Conventions

*

It is chastening to recall Egon Schwelb's testimony before the Subcommittee on International Organizations
and Movements of the House Foreign Affairs Committee in 1974. In his prepared statement, delivered two
years before the commitment of the U.S. to the international protection of human rights became an issue in
a presidential election campaign and before this commitment acquired a high profile in foreign policy statements of the United States, Dr. Schwelb said: "In the
narrower field of the international protection of human rights, the Dulles policy of 1953 is comparable to
the disaster which had happened 23 years earlier, when
the Senate did not assemble the two-thirds majority
which was required to give its consent to the ratification
of the Covenant of the League of Nations."[1] Though
the tone may seem a little apocalyptic, it reminds us
eloquently that while the issue of human rights may

1. *Hearings before the Subcomm. on International Organizations and
Movements of the House Comm. on Foreign Affairs*, 93d Cong., 1st Sess.
269, 278 (1973). Dr. Schwelb was a former deputy director of the
Division of Human Rights of the UN Secretariat.

have been given greater prominence by the present administration, the articulation of a general commitment—and the problems of its nonfulfillment—had been there for a long time. Indeed, as early as the establishment of the Atlantic Charter and of the Grand Alliance, the U.S. had participated in a commitment to a postwar international order that would take account of international concern for the protection of human rights. The UN Charter, with its provisions on human rights,[2] represents a manifestation of the new international order.

One of the most important activities of the UN has been the elaboration of the International Bill of Rights consisting of the Universal Declaration of Human Rights, the International Covenant on Economic, Social, and Cultural Rights, the International Covenant on Civil and Political Rights, and the Optional Protocol to the latter covenant.[3] The withdrawal in 1953 of the U.S. from the process of drafting these instruments and its continuing aloofness from participating in their operation demonstrate a degree of inconsistency that it is fair to say the U.S. must rectify if it is to maximize its declared commitment in favor of human rights, a commitment that we are assured is being sustained[4] and is "the soul" of American foreign policy.[5]

2. *See* U.N. CHARTER arts. 1(3), 55, 56, 62(2), 68, 73, 76.

3. A large number of specialized instruments have also been drawn up by the United Nations, one of the earliest of which was the Convention on the Prevention and Punishment of the Crime of Genocide (1948), which is also long overdue for ratification by the United States. These may be found conveniently assembled in UNITED NATIONS, HUMAN RIGHTS—A COMPILATION OF INTERNATIONAL INSTRUMENTS, ST/HR/1/Rev.1 (1978).

4. Derian, *The Carter Administration and Human Rights, Part II, A Commitment Sustained*, WORLDVIEW, July-August 1978, at 11–12.

5. Remarks by President Jimmy Carter, The White House Commemoration of the 30th Anniversary of the Universal Declaration of Human Rights 3 (December 6, 1978), *reprinted in 79* DEP'T STATE BULL. 2 (1979).

In *Word Politics*, a book designed to show the interaction of the Johnson and Brezhnev Doctrines and their mutually reinforcing effect, Professors Franck and Weisband wrote: "We intend that some readers conclude that any action by the United States which cannot be credibly set out in terms which build and strengthen a conceptual framework for the kind of reciprocally principled world we want can never be in our national interest."[6] Later in the book they said: "Unfortunately, the United States has never learned to listen to itself as if it were the enemy speaking."[7] Although the book had a specific focus, the underlying concern to demonstrate the importance of consistency in word and action in the charting of foreign policy remains applicable to other aspects of foreign policy, including that relating to the international promotion and protection of human rights.

I. *Disadvantages of Nonparticipation*

One of the disadvantages of nonparticipation in the promotion of human rights through the development of international standards became apparent when the U.S. opted out of the process of negotiating the texts of the international covenants on human rights.[8] But even where the U.S. has participated in the development of such standards, as for example in the conclusion of the Convention on the Elimination of All Forms of Racial Discrimination or, more recently, in the development of international standards (including a convention) against torture, the impact of that participation may well have been weakened by the possible perception on the part of representatives of other states that for the

6. T. FRANCK & E. WEISBAND, WORD POLITICS ix (1971).

7. *Id.* at 8.

8. This led to the abandonment of attempts to include a federal clause. *See Hearings, supra* note 1, at 278.

U.S. such activity is, in terms of future legal obligations, more academic than real.

Similarly, U.S. credibility is at stake in efforts to develop mechanisms to monitor compliance at the international level. The U.S. has taken strong and positive positions on the strengthening of the existing UN mechanisms providing for thorough studies or investigations of situations appearing to reveal consistent patterns of gross and reliably attested violations of human rights pursuant to Economic and Social Council Resolution 1503 (XLVIII). It has similarly sought to promote the establishment within the UN of a High Commissioner for Human Rights. Both of these efforts are designed to advance UN involvement in the protection of human rights by developing fact-finding techniques that would function on an objective basis. The development of such mechanisms would inhibit manipulation according to the preferences of fluctuating government majorities. Indeed, no delegation at the UN has been more vocal in the last few years than that of the U.S. in denouncing the apparent double standard with which the UN assesses various allegations of violations of human rights. Yet it is precisely the mechanisms established under the various international human rights instruments that are designed to institutionalize a more objective, consistent, and depoliticized approach to assessing such allegations. By standing aloof from participation in such UN human rights mechanisms, the credibility of the U.S. position is impaired when it eloquently complains about alleged double standards in actual UN investigations.

What is also damaging about the failure of the U.S. government to integrate itself into the standard-setting and compliance-assessment systems provided by the international instruments is that the U.S. opens itself to the charge that, despite concern for the protection of human rights in other countries, it is not willing to enter into an international obligation to protect human rights at home. You may not consider it a particularly fair argument or even a particularly cogent one, but as far as arguments go in the field of international politics it is an extremely telling one. Every time representatives of other countries introduce that argument in the UN or other international forums—and they often do so—they "score," and they would not continue this practice if they did not think they were scoring.

Of course, the damaging effect of noninvolvement in the international treaty protection systems is not just evident at the multilateral level; it also must inevitably limit the amount of influence the U.S. government can bring to bear bilaterally. This would be particularly true in the case of governments with which the U.S. does not already have a tradition of influence, especially of governments that have themselves ratified the instruments. When the Soviet Union, which has ratified, accuses the U.S. of exercising a double standard as a result of its nonratification, it is simply not a sufficient answer for the U.S. to retort that it only undertakes obligations that it intends to meet. For nonratification indicates either inability or unwillingness to comply with the obligation.

Indeed, the double-standard charge against the U.S. takes on particular significance in the context of some of the interesting legislation that has over the past few years been adopted by the Congress whereby U.S. aid policy is made subject to the taking into account of and compliance with"internationally recognized human rights."[9] There are a number of places one might go to look for internationally recognized human rights, but the International Bill of Rights, and not just the Declaration, would certainly be one such place. It can hardly

---

9. *See* Weissbrodt, *Human Rights Legislation and United States Foreign Policy*, 7 GA. J. INT'L & COMP. L. 231, 232 (1977).

enhance the integrity of the U.S. posture when it is prepared to incorporate into its own legislation standards
for application against others that it is not prepared to
apply juridically to itself.

Recognition of, and firm support for, the work of
nongovernmental groups in seeking to promote and
protect human rights has been a consistent and positive
hallmark of U.S. policy, particularly at the UN. Yet the
nonparticipatory position of the U.S. as far as the human rights conventions are concerned makes the efforts of the U.S. citizens working in such groups that
much more difficult. I recall that in 1973 or 1974 a
Swiss adoption group of Amnesty International received a letter from the then Solicitor General, Erwin
Griswold. The group had written to him on behalf of
one of its prisoners, an American conscientious objec-
tor to the Vietnam War. Having expressed admiration
for the work of Amnesty International, Dean Griswold
nevertheless asked how Swiss citizens coming from a
country that does not recognize the right to conscientious objection could presume to question the application of the U.S.'s selective service law. Of course, there
was a response to be made, not least that the Swiss section of Amnesty International was seeking to promote
change in the law in Switzerland to permit recognition
of the right to conscientious objection. But the argument used by Dean Griswold is telling. Similarly, when
members of Amnesty International USA write to governments that have ratified the covenants and indeed
may wish to invoke articles of the covenants in support
of their work, they may well have to face the reproach
that they come from a country that has not itself undertaken the same obligations as the authorities of the
country to which they are writing. Here too, these individuals will not be wholly deprived of a response; for
the very firm commitment of their own section of Amnesty International to securing ratification by the gov-

ernment of the U.S. represents at least a partial answer. How much easier and more effective their work would be if they could write as citizens of a nation that had now accepted the same legal obligations.

II. *The Advantages of Participation*

So far, I have concentrated on the disadvantages that flow from the U.S.'s nonratification of the major international human rights conventions. I shall now turn to the advantages that I see would flow from its ratification of the same conventions. Perhaps it goes without saying that the principal advantage would be avoidance of the disadvantages that I have already described. The major reproaches of inconsistency, hypocrisy, and the exercise of a double standard would lose their force.

At the close of the fifth session of the Human Rights Committee, Mr. Movchan, the expert from the Soviet Union, stated that "the Committee's deliberations had taken place in a friendly yet businesslike atmosphere, notwithstanding the many different legal systems in the countries of origin of its members. Its achievements constituted an outstanding example of international cooperation in the field of human rights."[10] This was the session of the Committee at which the report of the Soviet Union was examined and during which the representative from the Soviet government appearing before the Committee was subjected to close and probing questioning. There can be little doubt that in the two years of its existence, the Human Rights Committee, both in the development of its rules of procedure and in the manner in which it is following them, has surprised many seasoned observers of this aspect of UN work by its willingness to take its functions seriously. So far, one can detect a real intention to provide precisely

10. U.N. Doc. CCPR/C/SR.122 (1978).

the objective, impartial forum for human rights discussions that many accuse the UN of lacking. Of couse, it is too early to pronounce a final judgment. But what we have seen so far augurs well, and the same seems to be the case in respect of the Committee's work under the Optional Protocol—as far as one can tell from the inevitably laconic references in its reports to the confidential procedures under which the Protocol operates.

Nothing can be worse for the cause of human rights than that it be subsumed into the hostile posturings of interpower rhetoric. Instead of mutual declamations and denunciations, what we have with the covenants system is a forum and context for dialogue. I am not for a moment suggesting that the quiet exchanges of experts are the only, or necessarily even the best, means of protecting human rights. What I am saying is that they are an important means and a means that requires the development of an international consensus. I cannot help thinking that the U.S. like any other country and perhaps, as a major power, more than many countries—has much to gain from and to contribute to this new and developing institution.

More particularly, the U.S. may feel it has something to contribute to the work of the Committee. It could not have a governmental delegate on the Committee; that, indeed, is the Committee's strength. However, it would be one of the electors of the Committee, and it could nominate an expert who might be able to bring something of the rich tradition of American jurisprudence and legal creativity to bear upon the work of the Committee.[11]

Meanwhile, there would be far greater opportunities for U.S. participation in the appropriate forums of the

---

11. *See also* Schwelb, *Entry into Force of the International Covenants on Human Rights and the Optional Protocol to the International Covenant on Civil and Political Rights*, 70 AM. J. INT'L L. 511, 518–19 (1976).

UN in discussion of the annual reports of the Human Rights Committee. At the moment, any such participation by the U.S., or any other country that has not become a party to the covenant, is hardly likely to carry much weight, and when all is said and done it may well be that the long-term efficacy of the Committee will depend on how the General Assembly, to which the Committee reports through ECOSOC,[12] will react to the work of the Committee.

I do not hesitate to deal with what some would perceive to be the disadvantages of the U.S. being subjected to criticism by others in an international forum. This should indeed be listed amongst the manifest advantages of the U.S. being a party to the covenants and subject to the substantive and procedural obligations of those instruments. In my view, it is good for any and every country to be subjected to criticism. It is healthy and constructive, and this is so even if the criticism itself is not. For, in the final analysis, a forum for rational discussion of criticism, well- or ill-founded, is precisely the value that is afforded by the work of the Human Rights Committee. As I indicated earlier, there are no doubt areas of human rights where the U.S. would think it had reason to be fairly satisfied with its performance. I think there are other areas where that may not so easily be the case, and obviously here I have in mind to some extent the field of economic, social, and cultural rights. Of course, the examination of reports on these subjects under the appropriate covenant is subject to a different procedure. I am also mindful that, in various areas of civil and political rights, the history of the U.S., as of other countries, does not demonstrate continuous and uniform commitment to certain very fundamental civil and political rights. President Carter

12. 21 U.N. GAOR, Supp. (No. 16), U.N. Doc. A/6316, at 58 (1966) (Article 45).

has recently acknowledged that "the struggle for full human rights for all Americans—black, brown and white, male and female, rich and poor, is far from over."[13] Not only is there further to go, it is necessary to build safeguards against retrogression. Systematic international scrutiny is one such safeguard.

Any consensus of values that is in advance of the behavior it seems to regulate is inevitably also an international system of pressure. The fact that we are dealing with law rather than resolutions obviously intensifies the pressure. To borrow the language of a significant school of law, those who articulate claims under treaty standards will have a more insistent impact on the minds of the decision makers whose behavior is sought to be influenced or modified. In addition, the conventions in question all provide for greater or lesser degrees of structured examination of compliance with these standards. This not only increases pressure towards compliance, it is, of course, a process that deepens and further consolidates the developing international consensus that the mere words of the treaties already represent.

While, as I have indicated, a certain commitment to the promotion and protection of human rights at the international level has been the policy of successive U.S. administrations, it would be disingenuous not to recognize the qualitatively increased level of declared commitment by the present administration. One has to revert to the days of Eleanor Roosevelt to find the equivalent. But there is no guarantee that this level of commitment will be maintained in the future, and a great disservice could be done to the cause of the international promotion and protection of human rights were the U.S. to blow hot and cold on the issue accord-

13. Remarks by President Jimmy Carter, *supra* note 5.

ing to changes of administration. One does not have to be a cynic to appreciate that mere ratification of a number of treaties in the field can be no guarantee of a particular level of commitment. Nevertheless, it is a factor in establishing a structured involvement and participation in the field, and I consider that such participation by the U.S. would at least contribute to the institutionalization of a human rights commitment. The substantive scope and the structured procedures of the covenants may also contribute to the maturing and deepening of a policy conducted by an administration that does appear to wish to sustain its commitment.

It may also be cause for some satisfaction that what the U.S. does or does not do is frequently influential on the behavior of other countries. In the final analysis there can surely be no more desirable way to influence the behavior of others than by the example of one's own behavior. This is not mere rhetoric. I can assure you that in at least one Third World country it has been a matter of deep disappointment to those who are seeking to persuade their government of the importance of ratifying the covenants that the U.S. has itself not done so. It has been a partial answer that an administration of the U.S. has at least declared an intention to secure ratification. A complete answer would have been better. I should be surprised if there are not more countries in this category.

Another aspect of the same point is that there is reason to believe that the U.S. itself deems it desirable to encourage other countries to ratify international human rights instruments. The flood of ratifications of the American Convention of Human Rights in the year preceding its entry into force in July 1978 was, I suspect, at least encouraged by the U.S. How much more effective such activity would be, particularly outside the Caribbean region, if the U.S. could point to the fact that it too was prepared to abide by the same standards and procedures as those to which it was encouraging others to commit themselves.

III. *The Optional Protocol, American Convention, and the Convention on the Elimination of All Forms of Racial Discrimination*

So far, what I have said has focused largely on the covenants, although most of the remarks apply similarly to the other instruments submitted to the Senate for ratification. I shall just make a few brief remarks that are particularly pertinent to these instruments, as well as to one that has not been submitted. I start with the latter.

As regards the Optional Protocol, it is, in the view of Amnesty International, clearly necessary for states not only to become parties to the covenants themselves but to grant the right of individual petition. For any monitoring system to function effectively, it is ultimately necessary to have all the relevant information from all sources. In the field of human rights the victim is, of course, the primary source. In addition, this ensures that examination of the performance of individual countries is not determined either by the information—usually self-seeking—furnished by states submitting reports under the normal procedure of the covenants or by fluctuating political interest that may affect the operation of the interstate complaints procedure that is not yet in force. Of course, the introduction of the interstate complaints procedure is itself an advance over the reporting system, and it is to be welcomed that the U.S. has expressed an intention to make a declaration under Article 41 of the covenant. But, in the final analysis, objective monitoring requires free flow of information, which in turn requires the right of individual petition. I am happy to note that there would appear to be no objection in principle on the part of the administration to such a procedure, since that procedure is in fact inherent in the operation of the American Convention on Human Rights that has been submitted to the Senate for ratification. Further, I would think I would be remiss if I did not reaffirm the principle of the inherent desirability of providing individuals who think they have been victimized by their governments with a forum for bringing such alleged victimization to the attention of an international body. Many victims, in fact, may well wonder about what sort of a hearing they are likely to get before this UN body when they find out how limited their rights are under the covenant, how limited is the action that the Human Rights Committee can take, and that the deliberations take place behind closed doors. However, the individual right of petition is an advance.

As to the American Convention on Human Rights, it probably goes without saying that regional handling of problems is often more effective than treatment at the UN before the whole world community. Regional forums seem to commend themselves because of some mixture of cultural familiarity, political like-mindedness, and common juridical traditions, all of which lead to a greater measure of trust than might otherwise exist. There is a sense of dealing with a problem *en famille*. The Council of Europe has demonstrated the applicability of this approach to the field of human rights. Participation in the American Convention has, as I have already indicated, the added advantage of providing individuals with a direct and automatic right of complaint and with access to an international regional human rights instrumentality.

With regard to the Convention on the Elimination of All Forms of Racial Discrimination, it should be recognized that the whole question of racial discrimination— bound up as it is with the system of apartheid in South

Africa, not to mention the pervasive racial undertones underlying the recent period of colonialism—has become the benchmark of international human rights concern. In the humanitarian field, I doubt whether any international instrument, other than the Geneva Convention of 12 August 1949 on the Protection of Victims of War, has received the overwhelming amount of adherence that the Convention on the Elimination of All Forms of Racial Discrimination has. The Committee on the Elimination of Racial Discrimination (CERD) established by the convention has, over several years now, accomplished significant work that has in many respects provided a model for the early functioning of the Human Rights Committee established under the covenant. Some may feel that the civil rights movement of the 1960s achieved such results that the U.S. can now claim to be in substantial formal compliance with the provisions of the convention. However, the earlier history is so recent as to make it an act of particular symbolic importance for the U.S. to put a seal by treaty on the abandonment of its past behavior. Indeed, in one respect there is even room for leadership here. Insufficient declarations have been made under Article 14 of the convention, which permits individual petition to the CERD, to bring it into force. I note that no such declaration is contemplated in the letter of submittal contained in the President's message to the Senate. Such a declaration by the U.S. would have the effect of permitting it to take the initiative to persuade others to follow suit.

IV. *Declarations, Understandings, and Reservations*

I do not intend to deal in detail with the unseemly long lists of declarations, understandings, and reservations to the individual instruments contained in the

President's message.[14] But I could not conclude without making one or two brief general points on some of these. First of all, I note in the reservations a particular concern not to interfere with rights that are already constitutionally protected in the U.S. The first amendment rights of freedom of speech and of the press come particularly to mind. I wonder if the concerns reflected by these reservations are adequately founded in the light of Article 5, paragraph 2, of the Covenant on Civil and Political Rights: "There shall be no restriction upon or derogation from any of the fundamental human rights recognized or existing in any State Party to the present Covenant pursuant to law, conventions, regulations or customs on the pretext that the present Covenant does not recognize such rights or that it recognizes them to a lesser extent."[15]

As a representative of an organization that seeks the universal abolition of the death penalty, I feel obliged to say a word about the reservations on the articles concerning the right of life both of the covenant (Article 6) and of the American Convention (Article 4). And what I am about to say relates specifically to the death penalty and not to the right-to-life article of the American Convention. While the UN has proclaimed that the main objective to be pursued is the progressive reduction of the number of offenses for which the death penalty is applicable, with a view to the desirability of abolishing capital punishment,[16] one finds only fairly

14. *See* Weissbrodt, *United States Ratification of the Human Rights Covenants*, 63 MINN. L. REV. 35, 62–77 (1978).

15. The article bearing the same number in the Covenant on Economic, Social, and Cultural Rights makes substantially similar provision, as does Article 29 of the American Convention on Human Rights.

16. 32 U.N. GAOR, Supp. (No. 45), U.N. Doc. A/32/45, at 136 (1978).

weak safeguards of this position in the Covenant on
Civil and Political Rights. Slightly stronger ones are to
be found in the American Convention on Human
Rights. It is frankly amazing to find that the U.S. in
contemplating ratification of the covenant envisages
reservations that are even less stringent than these provisions and would permit the execution of pregnant
women under eighteen years of age. Of course, I am
aware of the problems of divided federal/state jurisdiction, but other reservations are envisaged in the President's message to cover that problem on other matters
covered by the conventions. What is required is that the
federal government take an abolitionist lead.

However difficult the internal political problem of
securing adherence to an international instrument, it
seems to be an utter misconception to assume that such
instruments are designed to improve the behavior of
others but only to confirm one's own status quo. It is to
be hoped that these instruments will improve the behavior of all, including that of the U.S. In brief, I should
like to support the view taken by the U.S. section of my
own organization, by the American Association for the
International Commission of Jurists, and by the International League for Human Rights to the effect that, as
a matter of policy, reservations should not be used to
limit freedoms and rights, but only to expand them.

Amnesty International works for the release of prisoners of conscience, and for fair trials within a reasonable time for all political prisoners, and against the
death penalty, torture, and cruel, inhuman, or degrading treatment or punishment in respect of all imprison-
oned human beings. Some of these victims may not be
covered explicitly by the various human rights conventions under consideration. Many will be. In the view of
Amnesty International, these individuals are being
wronged by their governments and ought to be able to
appeal to the organized international community. The

conventions are an important step in that direction. The greater the number of countries ratifying them, the greater will be the number of actual or potential victims able to benefit from them. These people should not be forgotten. The conventions will help ensure they are not.

LOUIS HENKIN

*   *   *

The Covenant
on Civil and
Political Rights

*

A full discussion of our subject might address a number of questions: Is ratification in the national interest? Are there any constitutional obstacles to ratification? Should we attach reservations, and if so, is there some principle of reservation to apply, or are there particular reservations we should impose? While perhaps not seemly to raise these questions here, one should consider also whether, if the President or the Senate insists on reservations we consider undesirable, we favor ratification nevertheless. An occasion like this might address also tactics for achieving ratification, tactics in discussions with the executive branch as well as with the U.S. Senate.

Some of the questions need not detain us long. I have little to add to what Nigel Rodley said about why it is in the interest of the U.S. to adhere. I would only stress that I have heard no reason for not adhering and that perhaps the strongest argument for adhering is that it will bring benefits and will cost nothing. The argument that adherence is undesirable because it would subject the U.S. to scrutiny, and to false accusations and distortions, is wholly unpersuasive. Our human rights record is subject to scrutiny whether we adhere or not. If there is valid criticism of us, we deserve it and should welcome it. False accusations and distortions may come and will have to be met whether or not we are a party. The Covenant on Civil and Political Rights, moreover, contains values with which we identify, and by which we try to live, and which are our most effective weapon in continuing ideological competition; it is particularly ironical that we have refused to adhere to it and that we now insist on attaching so many reservations to it.

I. *Constitutional Objections*

I can also dispose quickly of constitutional objections to ratification. In principle, there are no constitutional objections. The treaty makers can adhere to the human rights covenants. There are no constitutional objections based on federalism or the separation of powers or on some notion that the subject is not of international concern. Even Senator Bricker knew that 25 years ago; that is why he tried to amend the Constitution to make it impossible for us to adhere to such covenants. He knew that, if the Constitution were not amended, we could adhere to them. And the Constitution was not amended. In my view, even had he succeeded in amending the Constitution in the way that he wished, it still would not have barred our adherence to these particular conventions. But that does not matter now. The objections to ratification, then, are not constitutional but political, and even constitutional arguments are made principally for their political influence. The obstacle is an abiding and deep isolationism, and I am afraid that no reservations will meet that particular problem.

II. *Reservations*

As for the reservations proposed by the executive branch, I said that there were no constitutional obsta-

cles to adherence in principle. It may be necessary to
enter a reservation or to express an understanding as
regards Article 20, which provides that a state must
forbid war propaganda and advocacy of racial hatred.
Under our constitutional jurisprudence the U.S. could
prohibit such propaganda only if it incites to violence
or other unlawful action. A reservation or understanding to that article just about disposes of constitutional
problems.

The other proposed reservations are of a different
character. They do not reflect constitutional or other
objections to the substance of some article in the covenant. Rather, they represent three principles to which
the executive branch is committing itself for political
reasons. And the three principles cumulate, overlap,
and supplement each other. Any of them would just
about achieve the desired end, but the executive branch
suggests a triple approach.

What are these three principles? The first is that,
while the U.S. will adhere to this covenant, it will not
agree to any change in U.S. law as it is today. Mr. Rodley
referred to this as unseemly; I have called it ignoble
and have sometimes thought of it as outrageous. The
purpose of adhering to a treaty is to undertake obligations, in this case to adhere to a common international
standard. What sort of convention would you have if
every country adhered subject to the reservation that it
would not make any changes in its laws? If the Soviet
Union made such a reservation, we would, rightly, reject its adherence as fraudulent.

Some apparently support such a reservation with the
argument that it is necessary because it is unconstitu-
tional or undesirable to make changes in domestic law
by treaty. That is plain nonsense. We always have made
changes in domestic law by treaty. In fact, the framers
of the Constitution contemplated and desired that. If
one did not make domestic law by treaty, there would

be no sense in, no need for, a clause that declares treaties to be the supreme law of the land.

That first principle of reservation is, to put it mildly, undesirable. What is more, the second reservation, that these conventions shall not be self-executing, makes the first unnecessary. If the covenant will require legislation to give it effect, we would not be making law by treaty: all the changes made in the law would be made by the implementing legislation.

I am not insisting that one must accept every change the covenant would make in our law. I do say that we cannot refuse in principle to make any change. We should look at every change on its merits. I should add that, in fact, the covenant would make very few changes in U.S. law if we adhered without this first reservation. In most respects the covenant spells out what American rights are now and makes some others explicit. Students of constitutional law are always surprised to realize that there is no right to vote in the American Constitution, that there is no presumption of innocence, and that, looking at the text of the Constitution, the equal protection of the laws and freedom from racial and other invidious discrimination is required only of the states, not of the U.S. The U.S. cannot object to a document that says that it is also committed to equality. It would be nice to have a document that says we do not believe in torture; we do not have that in our Constitution—the Constitution forbids only cruel and unusual punishment, not torture or other forms of inhuman treatment not used as criminal punishment. The covenant forbids double jeopardy. In the U.S. we have a constitutional prohibition of double jeopardy, but it is not applicable when one of the "jeopardies" is by the state and one by the federal government. That was the result of a 5–4 decision by the Supreme Court [*Bartkus v. Illinois*, 359 U.S. 121 (1959)], but one could hardly insist that the opposite view, the one that the covenant

would presumably take, goes against the grain of our
Constitution. If Congress or a treaty decided to accept
the dissenting point of view in that case, I should have
thought most of us would be happy about it. This reservation is designed to prevent that. Noting another
proposed reservation, it certainly appears ludicrous for
the U.S. to reserve, in effect, the right to execute children and pregnant women.

Although we have lived with self-executing treaties
at least since John Marshall, the concept is still confused
in many minds, and it is not clear what making these
covenants non-self-executing will mean. Probably, it
will mean that the courts will not look to the treaties at
all. They will look only at any implementing legislation
that might be adopted. Of course, since—under the
first principle of reservation—the U.S. would refuse
any obligation to make any change in the current law,
why do you need to insist that the treaty is not self-
executing? There is nothing new to execute; no
changes are being made. If you should somehow wish
to conform to the international standard in some respect, you would have to repeat in both houses the political controversy that we anticipate in the Senate to
enact legislation to execute the covenant. And then, by
the way, if you have in mind the third reservation,
to which I am coming—the federal-state clause—you
might have to repeat that struggle fifty times more in
50 state legislatures. Again, it should be clear, I am not
objecting to having some particular clauses in the covenant left for legislative implementation, but why a blanket reservation requiring legislative implementation of
every clause?

The third reservation, as I have mentioned, is the so-
called federal-state clause. Again, unlike in Senator
Bricker days, nobody is prepared to argue today that
such a clause is constitutionally necessary. It is also un-

necessary and undesirable for other reasons. The efforts to draft federal-state clauses during the past 25 years have produced a dozen different versions. (The present one, I think, is the same as in the American Convention.) One of my objections to this reservation is that I simply do not understand it, and I must assume that the courts will have a little trouble with it too. On the one hand, it may have no effect and serve no purpose, in which case nothing will come of it. Or, if it serves a purpose, it will require implementation by fifty states and will presumably leave the U.S. in default unless these fifty states execute the obligations assumed by the U.S. Again, if there were some particular problem in which state autonomy is important, we ought to be willing to examine it. But this blanket obeisance to states' rights, or whatever one wishes to call it, seems to me an unnecessary confusion.

The executive branch, I am confident, has acted with great good will and tried to make the covenant palatable to Senators. Perhaps the Executive thought that one could split the opposition: if you take on all of them and give something to the states' rights people, something to those who believe laws should be made only by Congress, and something to those who insist we should not change American law to suit international standards, then you might get enough votes detached from that one-third opposition which could defeat ratification. My own view is that we ought to fight the opposition, not join them. I still hope we can persuade the Executive to move from these blanket reservations to a few precise ones, if any.

One word on tactics. I may be a heretic. If we have to take this treaty with these blanket reservations, I have serious doubts whether such ratification is better than none. But for now there is need for a big campaign for the covenant. That is the big job. We ought to focus on that job, on getting the covenant before the Senate, getting the Senators to adhere to the covenant in principle. At the same time, perhaps, we can work with or on the executive branch to rethink the reservations.

BURNS H. WESTON

* * *

U.S. Ratification of the International Covenant on Economic, Social and Cultural Rights
With or Without Qualifications

*

Like most of you—possibly all of you—I was thrilled when, at the outset of his tenure in the White House, President Carter chose to make the progressive achievement of international human rights a basic cornerstone of U.S. foreign (and domestic) policy. Even while recognizing the difficult compromises and trade-offs inevitably involved, I could only marvel at his March 1977 statement before the United Nations in which he declared this policy decision to be "not just a political posture" but "a commitment"; that is, an "[accepted] responsibility in the fullest and the most constructive sense."[1] And the more did I marvel when I thought about these words against the backdrop of his

Note: Professor Weston was not able to attend the conference. His paper was read by Mr. Hurst Hannum, whose own brief remarks follow Professor Weston's.
1. 76 DEP'T STATE BULL. 332 (1977).

27

inaugural address two months earlier, in which he
pledged the U.S. to "the elimination of all nuclear
weapons from this earth."² At long last, it seemed, my
country was going to stop treating international human
rights as essentially a footnote in the annals of world
history—maybe even to the point of recognizing that a
genuine commitment to international human rights is
not just a matter of altruism but also, and more importantly, a matter of enlightened self-interest and national security.

In the approximately two years since these stirring
presidential pronouncements, I have become deeply
disillusioned. Not that I think all is lost, else I would not
be sharing my thoughts with you here tonight; however, when I contrast President Carter's early statements with his February 23, 1978, letter to the Senate
transmitting for ratification the four human-rights
treaties that are the focus of this conference, I fear a
possible sellout. On top of certain dubious human
rights actions and decisions taken in the last two years,
the reservations, declarations, and statements of understanding accompanying President Carter's transmittal letter cause me to wonder whether he and his
administration are truly sincere about wanting to make
U.S. human rights policy more than "a political posture."

My concern is especially strong when it comes to the
International Covenant on Economic, Social, and Cultural Rights, which I shall refer to as the ECOSOC
covenant. Signed by President Carter on October 5,
1977, this covenant provides, as you all know, for the
progressive satisfaction (to the fullest extent possible
given available national resources) of a highly important cluster of both socioeconomic and cultural value

2. *Id.* at 122.

demands that go to the heart of the human condition, that go to the heart of human survival and the quality or dignity of life, including the right to gainful employment, to trade unionism, to social security, to an adequate standard of living (including adequate food, clothing, shelter, medical care, and critical social services), to education, to rest and leisure, and to participation in and enjoyment of the cultural, creative, and scientific life of one's society. In other words, except possibly for the UN Charter and the Universal Declaration of Human Rights, this covenant represents the first large-scale effort in international legal history to translate the language of socioeconomic *needs* into the language of socioeconomic *rights*; and, for the overwhelming majority of the people of this planet, this development obviously constitutes a major and long-awaited departure in the history of human affairs.

Yet, despite this fact and the worldwide expectations attendant upon it, and despite a long-standing (even if not always well-executed) tradition on the part of the U.S. to ensure the survival and basic needs of individual human beings everywhere (a tradition whose origins date back to the birth of our Republic), the Carter Administration has proposed a series of qualifications to the ECOSOC covenant that, in my judgment, tend to undermine, even to emasculate, the purposes for which this covenant—and, indeed, our Republic—stand. International customary law does, of course, attach different legal significance or consequence to such qualifications depending on the labels used; but, when viewed as a whole, and in several instances in particular cases, their net impact is, I believe, depressing and regrettable.

So in the remainder of my remarks I would like to consider these qualifications, or commitment withdrawals—for that is exactly what they are—and to pro-

pose what I think should be done about them. They
include two reservations, three understandings, and
two declarations, including one combined declaration
and understanding.

I. *The Two Reservations*

A. *Free Speech*

The first proposed reservation pertains to Article
5(1) of the ECOSOC covenant, which provides that
"[n]othing in the present Covenant may be interpreted
as implying for any State, group or person, any right to
engage in any activity or to perform any act aimed at
the destruction of any of the rights or freedoms recognized herein, or at their limitation to a greater extent
than is provided for in the present Covenant. Correctly,
the Carter Administration has perceived a potential
conflict with the First Amendment free-speech guarantees of our Constitution. Accordingly, because a
treaty cannot be ratified by the Senate if it conflicts
with the Constitution,[3] the administration has recommended the following reservation: "[T]hat nothing in
this Covenant shall be deemed to require or to authorize legislation or other action by the United States
which would restrict the right of free speech protected
by the Constitution, laws, and practice of the United
States." The trouble with this reservation is that, while
appropriate in referring to the Constitution, it goes too
far in referring also to the "laws and practice of the
United States."

In the first place, this additional reference is unnecessary. Free speech laws and practices in the U.S. are
constitutionally protected; therefore, they would be
protected by a reservation limited in reference to the

3. Kinsella v. United States *ex rel.* Singleton, 361 U.S. 234, 248
(1960).

U.S. Constitution only. Secondly, as our colleague David Weissbrodt from the University of Minnesota has recently pointed out, this additional reference could be used perversely to authorize U.S. "laws and practice" that would be *less* protective of free speech than Article 19 of the International Covenant on Civil and Political Rights. Because Article 19 could be interpreted to prohibit "laws and practice" that heretofore have been sanctioned by our Supreme Court—for example, authorization of police surveillance of peaceful demonstrations—the proposed reservation actually may offer less free-speech protection than is afforded by the covenants. Accordingly, the reservation could be used to prevent any treaty-based improvement in U.S. laws and practice.

In sum, insofar as the free speech reservation refers to "laws and practice of the United States," it is superfluous and probably very shortsighted. Furthermore, because it signals to the world that we will abide by the covenant so long as such adherence does not require any improvement in our own free speech practices, it encourages other countries to make similar status quo reservations—reservations that, in turn, would seriously jeopardize the protection of free speech as envisioned in the Civil and Political Covenant. Therefore, the proposed reservation should be revised so as to exclude reference to the "laws and practice of the United States."

B. *States' Rights*

The second reservation pertains to Article 28 of the ECOSOC covenant, which stipulates that "the provisions of the present Covenant shall extend to all parts of federal States without any limitation or exceptions." According to the Carter Administration, which seems to fear some violation of states' rights or some inconsistency with our federal system, this provision requires the following reservation:

> The United States shall progressively implement all the provisions of the Covenant over whose subject matter the Federal Government exercises legislative and judicial jurisdiction; with respect to the provisions over whose subject matter constituent units exercise jurisdiction, the Federal Government shall take appropriate measures, to the end that the competent authorities of the constituent units may take appropriate measures for the fulfillment of this Covenant.

In short, the Carter Administration would limit the impact of the covenant on state governments within the U.S.

In thus proceeding, however, the Carter Administration has forgotten our constitutional history and consequently has reopened old wounds. In a phrase, this proposed states' rights reservation constitutes a legal/historical anachronism. In addition to the fact that the U.S. Supreme Court has unequivocally upheld the power of the federal government to make treaties in respect of matters that otherwise would be the sole perogative of the separate states,[4] the recent trend of constitutional decision, at least since the early 1950s, has been to resolve virtually all states' rights doubts in favor of federal power—via the commerce clause and via the thirteenth, fourteenth, and fifteenth amendments. Moreover, there is absolutely no question that the U.S. government has the authority to enter into human rights treaties per se.

But the real objection to the proposed states' rights reservation is that it could be not just a silly anachronism but a *costly* one, both domestically and internationally. Domestically, there is the possibility that it would

4. Missouri v. Holland, 252 U.S. 416 (1920).

refuel politically retrogressive (perhaps even racist) divisions that, in turn, could call into question even the limited international human rights commitments that have so far been made by the U.S. And internationally, because the reservation is so explicitly contrary to the language and intent of Article 28, it could vitiate the covenant in major part. Under traditional international law, such a reservation to a treaty, which is analogous to a counteroffer to a contract, must be accepted by all parties for the treaty to be considered binding. Thus, assuming that the states' rights reservation were to be perceived—as well it might—as fundamentally incompatible with Article 28, it could be legitimately maintained that no agreement has been reached and therefore no binding treaty established.

As I see it, then, the proposed states' rights reservation should be ruled out entirely. So also should any equivalent alternatives, since the matter of federalism, especially in the human rights field, is best left up to our courts on a case-by-case basis.

II.   *The Three Undertakings*

A.   *Progressive Implementation*

In contrast to the Civil and Political Covenant, which speaks in less futuristic terms, Article 2(1) of the ECO-SOC covenant provides that "[e]ach State Party . . . undertakes to take steps, individually and [collectively] . . . with a view to achieving progressively the full realization of the rights recognized" by the covenant. The Carter Administration's stipulated understanding of this provision is that Articles 1 through 15 of the covenant "describe goals to be achieved progressively rather than through immediate implementation." In the end, this proposed understanding might prove only redundant, and therefore harmless for being superfluous.

However, by adding the language of nonimmediacy—
i.e., "rather than through immediate implementation"—
it is possible that it could be interpreted to justify unwarranted delays, much too deliberate speed, in taking
immediate steps toward the progressive achievement
of the goals enumerated. Also, at the very least, it com-
municates an embarrassing foot-dragging that scarcely
is in keeping with a full and constructive commitment
to the human rights cause. Accordingly, the understanding should be dropped entirely.

B. *Foreign Aid*

Again with reference to Article 2(1) of the ECOSOC
covenant, the Carter Administration asserts an understanding that the covenant does not require foreign
economic aid when it obligates each State Party "to take
steps, individually and through international assistance
and cooperation . . . to the maximum of its available
resources, . . . [and] by all appropriate means" toward
the progressive realization of the rights enumerated.
Because Article 2(1) does not actually impose a duty to
give foreign economic aid, this understanding surely
would instill or reinforce an impression of Scrooge-like
churlishness on the part of the U.S. in relation to the
meeting of basic human needs, and it provides unfortunate grist for the anti-American propaganda mill.
This proposed understanding, too, should be stricken
from the record.

C. *Citizenship Discrimination*

The third and final understanding proposed by the
Carter Administration relates to Article 2(2) of the
ECOSOC covenant forbidding discrimination in implementation of the covenant on the basis of "race, colour,
sex, language, religion, political or other opinion, national or social origin, property, birth or other status."

The proposed understanding is that this language "permits reasonable distinctions based on citizenship"— for instance, in ownership of land or of means of communication (two examples expressly mentioned in the Carter transmittal message). Presumably, this proposed understanding is designed to protect domestically based U.S. industries and assets from foreign control. This seems clear. Not so clear, however, is how one should respond to it—bearing in mind that, if retained, it would invite equivalent and probably even more far-reaching understandings from other States Parties to the Covenant. The answer, I believe, must necessarily depend on one's views about the global economic system. If one believes that it is desirable to foster conditions conducive to direct U.S. capital investment abroad, particularly in the developing world where anti-U.S. and anticapitalist sentiment may be strong, then probably the understanding should be discarded—because, as we say, what is sauce for the goose is sauce for the gander. If, on the other hand, one believes that the export of U.S. capitalism is not always or even usually in the best interests of the host countries involved, then probably it should be retained. The decision here is more ideological than legal.

III. *The Two Declarations*

A. *Private Property Rights*

Article 2(3) of the ECOSOC covenant provides that "[D]eveloping countries, with due regard to human rights and their national economy, may determine to what extent they would guarantee the economic rights recognized in the present Covenant to nonnationals." In addition, Article 25 provides that nothing in the covenant "shall be interpreted as impairing the inherent right of all peoples to enjoy and utilize fully and freely their natural wealth and resources."

In response to these two provisions, the Carter Administration proposes the following combined declaration and understanding: "The United States declares that nothing in the Covenant derogates from the equal obligation of all States to fulfill their responsibilities under international law. The United States understands that under the Covenant everyone has the right to own property alone as well as in association with others, and that no one shall be arbitrarily deprived of his property." In other words the right to own private property, one of the fundamental—and often stridently espoused—tenets of U.S. law and policy, is given special protection.

Of course, there can be no objection to requiring all states to fulfill their responsibilities under international law. However, considering the dangers of ethnocentrism, I have serious misgivings when it comes to insisting that "everyone has the right to own property," particularly in an increasingly ideologically divided world. Also, for similar reasons, I have misgivings about the Department of State's express gloss on the declaration, namely, that "under international law, any taking of private property . . . must be accompanied by prompt, adequate, and effective compensation." My point is that the international law of state responsibility, early fashioned by a Western capital-exporting world and now subject to the pressures of a Third World movement for a "new international economic order," is changing rapidly. It is by no means clear that the Department's views of international law in this realm are today either accurate or justified.

On the other hand, given the exemption extended to the "developing countries" under Article 2(3) of the covenant, some safeguards do seem justified. The ultimate purpose of international legal decision—and so, international human rights decision—is and should be the reconciliation and accommodation of competing points of view and interests. Accordingly, I would revise the Carter Administration's property rights declaration and understanding to read as follows: "The United States declares that nothing in the Covenant derogates from the equal obligation of all States to fulfill their responsibilities under international law relative to foreign private wealth ownership, including the duty to ensure that no one shall be arbitrarily deprived of his property." Such a declaration, I believe, would be judiciously appropriate.

B. *Non-Self-Executing Treaty*

Finally, despite a constitutional supremacy clause tradition that says that treaties, as part of the supreme law of our land, may sometimes be considered applicable by the courts without special implementing legislation, the Carter Administration proposes to declare that "the provisions of Articles 1 through 15 of the ECOSOC Covenant are not self-executing." More than any other qualifying statement, this one, in my view, does the most harm. In effect, it emasculates the covenant (the more so when it is seen in conjunction with the non-immediate-implementation understanding mentioned earlier). Contrary to the language of the covenant that conveys a clear self-executing intent, in particular as regards the obligation to take steps toward the progressive realization of the rights enumerated, the proposed declaration would require intermediate legislative action to implement the covenant's provisons, and, accordingly, the covenant would have little or no effect beyond that of a lofty policy pronouncement. No one could sue in court to enforce its provisions; no one could use the covenant as a source of genuinely binding law. For these and related reasons, therefore, this declaration should be stricken—assuming, that is, that it is not already too late. By attempting to remove the issue of the self-executing nature of the covenant from the courts, where traditionally this issue ultimately has resided, President Carter may have given away too much too soon and thereby have dealt a severe blow to the human rights movement with which he has become so closely identified.

IV. *Conclusion*

To sum up, most, if not all, the reservations, understandings, and declarations proposed by the Carter Administration can be seen to be either superfluous, churlish, violative of international law, contrary to enlightened self-interest, or a combination of all. As such, in my view, they reflect an administration that is either legally and politically naive or not genuinely interested in the constructive pursuit of economic, social, and cultural rights worldwide.

In any event, let us hope that the U.S. Senate will be much, much wiser; and let us do all we can to ensure that it will be. The time is long overdue for economic, social, and cultural rights to be accorded the same dignity and status we in the West have been wont to give to civil and political rights. By ratifying the ECOSOC covenant without abundant qualification, the Senate would be telling an incredibly poverty-stricken world that the U.S. believes as much in abolishing the economic exploitation and social oppression that have tended to characterize developed capitalism as it does in abolishing the political repression and authoritarian practices that have tended to characterize state socialism. Few other things could be done that would enhance our global image and credibility more.

HURST HANNUM

* * *

Comments

*

I am certainly in general agreement with Professor Weston's remarks. However, I do not share his concern on several issues. First, on the issue of whether the covenant is self-executing, I think there is confusion between whether the treaty creates a legal obligation and whether its provisions are self-executing, *i.e.*, its provisions are to be enforced directly by domestic tribunals. It is clear from reading the instrument that it does require domestic legislation for its implementation; its terms are simply not specific enough to be directly enforceable in our courts. Therefore, to the extent that the reservation focuses on the non-self-executing nature of the treaty, it does not pose a serious problem. The important point is that the treaty does create a binding legal obligation on the U.S. to make progress toward the goals embodied in the convention.

Second, I think that there should have been another speech made at this symposium and that speech should have addressed whether the U.S. Senate should approve these instruments at all, given the reservations that have been attached to them by the administration. While I will admit to being a devil's advocate on this point, and that I have not made up my mind on this position, it certainly does seem to be the case that human rights proponents may be "giving away the game" by accepting these instruments with the reservations we now are discussing. As there will be no nongovernment

speaker on this panel who will argue that the reservations are uniformly desirable, most remarks will be addressed to changing the reservations, to deleting some
of the understandings, and to making the covenants
more reasonable. If these things could be achieved, I
would certainly support ratification; however, I do not
think that we must take anything that we are given. If
these treaties are presented for final vote in the Senate
with all of the reservations that are attached now, all of
us on this panel must question whether the treaties
should be approved at all. The reservations are not
going to be changed; none of them will be withdrawn
in the future when we have a more enlightened foreign
policy either in the administration or the Senate. Those
of us who could be considered on the left of these issues
should not be taken for granted; it is a dangerous position to take that these treaties should be ratified under
any circumstances.

Mr. Rodley referred to some of the advantages that
would accrue from U.S. ratification. The most important of these is that the U.S. will be able to participate in
various international institutions that monitor violations, and it will have an opportunity to contribute to
the development of international human rights law.
However, I am not convinced that ratification of these
treaties with their present reservations will do anything
at all for the development of human rights in this country. In fact, the attitude expressed in the President's
message indicates that the reservations represent a
hypocritical paranoia.

CLYDE FERGUSON

*   *   *

International Convention on the Elimination of All Forms of Racial Discrimination

*

Ten years ago when we addressed the problem of ratifying the covenants about which I am *not* speaking at
this meeting, I suggested that we should separate the
legal issues—constitutional and international—from issues of will. I would like to make a few comments about
the origin of the International Convention on the
Elimination of All Forms of Racial Discrimination [con-
vention] as it may be relevant to will—will that has been
expressed, perhaps with faint praise, in the President's
transmittal letter to the Senate.

First, the convention was adopted in December 1965,
just two years after the General Assembly adopted the
Declaration on the Elimination of All Forms of Racial
Discrimination [declaration]. I think it significant that
eighteen years intervened between the Universal Declaration of Human Rights and the General Assembly's
adoption of the two covenants. Second, unlike the lack
of U.S. participation in the drafting of the covenants,
there was very active participation on the expert level
by two U.S. citizens in the Subcommission on Discrimination. This emphasizes the importance of full participation by the U.S. in the drafting of international

41

instruments, and in the developing of institutions that
will be at least partially responsible for implementation.
Hence, I suspect that in the convention we have an instrument that, when compared to the covenants, is a
better document in terms of U.S. interest, the expression of U.S. values, and the expression of the U.S. view
about what should be done to eliminate racial discrimination. It did not deserve the reservations, declarations, understandings, and construction that it received
from the Executive.

I think that it is useful to recall that the brief period
between the declaration and the adoption of the convention was the result of two worldwide forces that had
a unique impact in the U.S. One of these forces was
clearly the emergence of the newly independent Afri-
can nations in the UN. These nations were, in one
sense, disappointed at what appeared to be the record
in dealing with issues of high priority to them: the
length of time required to draft human rights covenants and the ideological dispute between the West,
which maintained that freedom comes from limitations, and the East, which held that freedom results
from establishing conditions. Their disappointment
served as an impetus to the UN to change its direction,
to begin to look at problems like racial discrimination,
and to recognize the need for the present convention.
The political force of these Third World nations is still
of great interest, concern, and importance to the U.S.

The second of these forces was, of course, the fact
that the convention was drafted in the middle of the
civil rights movement from 1962–65. There are provisions in the convention that emanated directly from the
American experience. For example, after Mr. Roy Wil-
kins testified before the Senate Judiciary Committee
about the difficulty blacks encountered traveling in the
South and about their being excluded from hotels, res-

taurants, and public places, the drafting group developed a provision, which appears to be out of order in the convention, relating to the right of access to all places of public accommodation. That is a reflection of the American experience, and it came before our domestic omnibus bill. Also, with the exception of the provisions in the convention dealing with economic and social rights, there appears to be a very close relationship between the convention and our Civil Rights Act of 1964. The relationship is not wholly accidental; to a large degree, it represents the effect of U.S. participation as well as an international acceptance of the norms embodied in the Civil Rights Act.

I would like to discuss briefly the major features of the convention. First, the convention is comprehensive as it applies to discrimination in public life; however, *public life* is subject to Executive construction. This construction probably corresponds to the intent of the drafters of the convention to comprehend something like our conception of state action, and to reserve some area of privacy where racially offensive notions do not have the capacity to injure others. Although there may be other views as to the difference between *public* and *private*, or the scope of *public discrimination*, as that term is used in the convention, it is clear that the word *public* was certainly intended to cover cases—whether or not there was state action—where there were public functions or where public places, or the like, practiced discrimination.

Second, apart from the comprehensive nature of the convention in a limited field, certain civil and political rights are set out, and their presence is, as Professor Henkin has observed, the emanation of the Western notion that freedom comes from imposing restrictions on the government. Unlike those rights in the two covenants, the economic, social, and cultural rights in the convention are not goals to be realized progressively, but are rights already in existence that the state undertakes not to deny its citizens on the basis of race.

Tactically speaking, the reservations, declarations, and understandings that have been appended to all of the instruments that we are discussing at this meeting are a disappointment to those of us interested in the field. However, it is especially disappointing that the Executive should claim that the convention, which was drafted with U.S. participation and which has at least some of its roots in our Civil Rights Act of 1964, is a non-self-executing instrument. This position derives from some concern that implementation of the convention would pose First Amendment problems. Although one may certainly not object to a concern to protect freedom of expression, the broad reservation that has been appended to the convention is unnecessary, because we cannot undertake international legal obligations that are beyond our constitutional power. In any event, the breadth of the reservation should be limited to the First Amendment concerns that the reservists had in mind, and it should not cover the concern for the prevention of the incitement of racial violence—a necessary and desirable thing for our society.

There is also a federal-state reservation, about which I have stronger feelings. I would have thought that some of these issues had been resolved by the Civil War and that it was no longer necessary to deal with the matter as the reservation does. The transmittal letter discusses two provisions that, incidentally, also emanated from the U.S. civil rights experience. These provisions deal with special measures that may be taken by States Parties to improve the condition of certain groups that have been the subject of discrimination in the past. The transmittal letter is accurate in characterizing these provisions as involving "affirmative action." These two provisions in the convention—Article 1(4) and Article 2(2)—derive directly from an opinion of the general counsel of the Civil Rights Commission in April 1963, which concerned the withholding of federal funds from certain states that were using those funds to aid discrimination in some sense. The notion of affirmative action originates in the Constitution. The provisions of the convention state that States Parties will engage in affirmative action when a determination is made that such action is warranted; I would object to any construction of these provisions under which the duty to act affirmatively to rectify past discrimination is not of a mandatory and immediate nature. I am aware that these provisions involve sensitive issues about which there will be a sharp division of opinion.

Finally, I think that my government colleagues, whom I know to be people of good will, are stressing acceptability to the Senate to the point of giving away the game and, perhaps inadvertently, of resurrecting Bricker Amendment debates that I would have thought were laid to rest long ago. Recent research has indicated that the real steam behind the Bricker Amendment was a fear that foreigners in New York would write an international civil rights bill that would become effective in the U.S. That civil rights bill came to pass in the form of the convention. The Bricker Amendment was fueled in the first instance by a case decided in an appellate court in California, which dealt with the ownership of property. The case struck down the California statute, and in doing so, it referred not only to the U.S. Constitution and the California Constitution but also to the Universal Declaration of Human Rights. Second, in the restrictive covenants cases, the NAACP filed a brief that referred to the Universal Declaration of Human Rights and the right to own property as being a right binding in international law. Third, the U.S. did not participate in the drafting of the covenants, and it is at least arguable that the right to own property is not included in the convenants. Those three things, at least two of which have quite clear racial overtones, are the real roots of the Bricker Amendment.

I fear that we face another searing national debate because of the submission of the two covenants and of this convention replete with reservations, declarations, understandings, and questionable constructions.

THOMAS BUERGENTHAL

*   *   *

The American Convention on Human Rights

*

Most of the reservations proposed in the President's letter of transmittal for the two covenants and the Racial Convention are also being proposed for the American Convention. My subject has consequently been covered to a large extent by the speakers who preceded me. That being the case, my comments relating to the reservations will be brief. Instead, I would like to devote most of my time to a discussion of the American Convention and the reasons why I deem it very important that the U.S. ratify this treaty.

There is talk that it is unlikely that the U.S. will ratify the American Convention in the foreseeable future. This speculation is based on the fact that the convention has a provision bearing on the politically sensitive abortion issue. (American Convention, Article 4[1]). I hope that those making this prediction are as wrong as some of us were when we predicted a few years ago that it would take decades for the American Convention to enter into force. As you know, it entered into force in July 1978 and has now been ratified by fourteen OAS member states.

The American Convention differs in a number of important respects from the human rights treaties that the other speakers have dealt with tonight. The most significant difference is that the American Convention,

in addition to guaranteeing a lengthy catalog of civil
and political rights, provides for the establishment of
two bodies—a court and a commission—having extensive judicial and quasi-judicial powers. Unlike the other
instruments we have been talking about, the American
Convention establishes a relatively complete system for
the protection of civil and political rights. It is a system
modeled in large measure on the European Convention of Human Rights, but is, in many ways, better
suited than that treaty for dealing with the problems of
the Western Hemisphere.

The Inter-American Commission on Human Rights
provided for by the American Convention will take the
place of the present Inter-American Commission. The
present commission has a very respectable track record
and performs useful investigatory functions. Under
the convention and the specific language in the revised
OAS Charter, the new commission will retain the powers of the present commission with regard to all OAS
member states, whether or not they have ratified the
convention. And it acquires additional powers—investigatory and quasi-judicial powers—with regard to the
States Parties to the convention.

One of the interesting innovations of the American
Convention is the manner in which it deals with the
right of individual petition. By merely ratifying the
convention, each State Party to the convention is
deemed to have accepted the right of the commission
to act on individual petitions charging the State Party
with a violation of the convention. But before interstate
communications—that is, complaints by one State Party
against another—can be heard by the commission, the
states involved have to have recognized the commission's jurisdiction to do so. In other words, the American Convention provides for a mandatory right of
private petition to the commission and makes the interstate complaint optional, which is just the reverse of the

system established by the European Convention. Experience indicates that, on the whole, the right of private petition is vital to an effective system for the protection of human rights. For dealing with massive violations of human rights, however, the inter-state complaint machinery provides greater political leverage; states should therefore be encouraged to recognize it by making the optional declaration. In his letter of transmittal, President Carter does in fact propose to make this declaration on behalf of the U.S., and that is a very important and wise step indeed.

Unlike the provisions relating to the right of private petition found in the Optional Protocol to the Covenant on Civil and Political Rights and the optional clause of the Racial Convention, the individual petition system established under the American Convention provides for quasi-judicial proceedings, hearings, and investigations and for a final adjudicative determination by the commission. Furthermore, judicial review by the Inter-American Court of Human Rights is also possible in certain cases.

With regard to OAS member states that are not parties to the convention, the convention commission retains, as I already noted, the powers of the present commission, which include the right to carry out country investigations as well as a limited power to deal with individual complaints. It is clear, however, that if certain major countries in the hemisphere do not become parties to the convention as such, political forces in the OAS not friendly to human rights in general will find it easier to limit the preexisting powers of the commission or, at the very least, to prevent their gradual expansion. Thus, for example, if the U.S. does not ratify the convention, our political involvement in the American Convention system will, of necessity, decrease, as will our influence. It is public knowledge that strong U.S. lobbying convinced many OAS member states to ratify the convention, thus making it possible for this instrument to enter into force. This lobbying effort was undertaken on the theory, with which I agree, that the existence of an effective OAS human rights system will significantly reduce the need for unilateral measures by the U.S. against countries in the hemisphere that violate human rights, thereby helping to depoliticize the promotion of human rights in the Americas. If we do not ratify the convention, become part of this system, and have a direct stake in it, then the whole fabric that the U.S. labored so hard to weave could rapidly come apart again.

Some institutional aspects of the American Convention amount to highly practical innovations. A good example is provided by the advisory jurisdiction powers conferred on the Inter-American Court of Human Rights. The Inter-American Court has dual jurisdiction: it has contentious jurisdiction, *i.e.*, jurisdiction to decide a specific dispute in which a State Party is charged with a violation of the convention, and it also has advisory jurisdiction. The contentious jurisdiction is optional and applies only to states that, in addition to ratifying the convention, have also recognized the court's jurisdiction. Thus far only one state—Costa Rica—has made this optional declaration.

The court's advisory jurisdiction, on the other hand, is very broad, quite novel, and important. For one thing, the court has power to render advisory opinions at the request of any OAS member state, whether or not that state has ratified the convention. Secondly, all OAS organs—whether it be the General Assembly, the Council, the Commission on Women, or the Inter-American Commission on Human Rights—may seek advisory opinions from the court. Finally, the advisory jurisdiction of the court applies to the interpretation not only of the convention but also of "other treaties concerning the protection of human rights in the

American states" (Art. 64). An imaginative use of this advisory jurisdiction power could lay the groundwork within the OAS for a human rights lawmaking process capable of avoiding the political friction that unfavorable court judgments in contentious cases tend to produce. Here, in my opinion, we have a unique institutional framework for developing a viable legal mechanism for the promotion of human rights in the Americas.

If I had the time, I could cite many other examples showing that the American Convention is a human rights treaty very much needed and is deserving of speedy U.S. ratification. Let me merely emphasize that it provides the U.S. with a unique opportunity to participate in the building of an important regional system for the protection of human rights that could also become a model for other regions of the world. At the same time, I doubt very much that without full U.S. participation the inter-American system will realize its full potential, and that would be a great pity indeed.

Now to the reservations. Let me note, first, that the American Convention contains a federal-state clause similar to that being proposed by the U.S. for the other conventions. No U.S. reservation on this subject is therefore proposed. What is proposed are a number of specific declarations and reservations, in addition to the declaration making the substantive provisions of the convention non-self-executing. If this declaration is accepted and upheld by U.S. courts, it would have the effect of preventing our courts from applying the convention. The consequences would be particularly detrimental in the context of the American Convention, whose commission and court will thus be unable to benefit from U.S. court decisions interpreting the convention, and vice versa. That is, the creative interaction between international and domestic courts, which has greatly enhanced the contribution and value of the European Convention, would be lost as far as the U.S. is concerned. What bothers me most about the attitude reflected in this approach is that the U.S. is sacrificing a tremendous opportunity when it comes to developing international human rights law, for the declaration will prevent our courts, with their long experience in human rights, from participating in and interacting with the lawmaking process on a regional plane. That is much too high a price to pay to placate the remnants of some Bricker Amendment supporters.

As for the other reservations or declarations, they are for the most part either justified or at least not seriously objectionable. Of course, I also disagree with the philosophy that attaches a reservation to each provision of a human rights treaty that does not conform to a country's domestic law. That is a form of know-nothing arrogance that does not advance the cause of human rights, to which the U.S. is presumably committed. There are a few reservations that, I think, are so petty or unnecessary that I wonder whether they should not be dropped as undignified for a country like ours.[1] I also believe, of course, that we should recognize the jurisdiction of the Inter-American Court of Human Rights. The U.S. is usually among the first countries to complain about the politicization of international and regional human rights procedures, yet when an opportunity exists, as it does in the case of the Inter-American Court, to place the system on a sound legal foundation by recognizing the court's jurisdiction, our government is unwilling to grasp the opportunity.

Finally, I would like to make one point on the issue of reservations, particularly those relating to specific pro-

1. *See, e.g.,* proposed declaration on Art. 22, para. 8, Letter of Submittal from the Department of State to the President (December 17, 1977), *reprinted in* MESSAGE FROM THE PRESIDENT OF THE UNITED STATES TRANSMITTING FOUR TREATIES PERTAINING TO HUMAN RIGHTS, S. EXECUTIVES C,D,E,& F, 95th Cong., 2d Sess. xxi (1978).

visions. I would much rather see the U.S. ratify these conventions with reservations than having the U.S. not ratify them at all. There is a risk that those opposing these conventions altogether will argue that if we can only ratify them with numerous reservations, we should not do it at all, particularly if other countries have attached only a few reservations. The argument will be that "it looks bad to have so many reservations." We will look even worse by staying out altogether. We will also be able neither to contribute to nor to benefit from these treaties. So let us ratify—without many reservations, if possible; with many reservations, if necessary. But let us ratify.

ARTHUR ROVINE

*   *   *

Defense of Declarations, Reservations, and Understandings

*

First, I want to say that this administration certainly wants these human rights treaties. I agree with almost everything that Nigel Rodley said about the damage that is being done to the U.S. by our failure to approve the treaties, as well as other important human rights instruments. There are others as well. We have not heard much mention tonight of the Genocide Convention, which has been sitting in the Senate for almost thirty years and has been reported out no less than four times by the Foreign Relations Committee. It has yet to be debated on the merits on the floor of the Senate. That, too, I think is a great pity. We are committed to these treaties, and we are hopeful that we will have them.

The Optional Protocol, another treaty that we have not become a party to, and which has not been signed, is worth a brief mention. We have not signed it because a judgment was made that it would probably do more damage in the Senate to the other treaties than it would do good. Whether that judgment was correct or not, I do not know. But we have no objection in principle to the Optional Protocol. We have agreed to its approach in other contexts, such as the Inter-American Convention on Human Rights and the Racial Discrimination

Convention. It was feared that if the Optional Protocol were sent over at this time, it might bring down the rest of the human rights treaties in the Senate. Another way of looking at it, however, is that it might have been the lightning rod to take all the heat and perhaps make it a bit easier for the other treaties to go through. I am not certain; a judgment call was involved, and I am hopeful that the Optional Protocol will, in due course, be signed and submitted to the Senate.

With regard to the treaties that we have submitted, and the recommended reservations and understandings, it is important to emphasize that we are working with a difficult political setting; I do not think that has been given sufficient attention by the panelists here tonight. As you know, there is a certain reluctance in the Senate to approve human rights treaties. And you might ask, "Why is that so?" What is so difficult about a human rights treaty that the Senate cannot bring itself to approve that instrument unless it is completely innocuous, such as the 1953 Convention on the Political Rights of Women—which was approved not too long ago, and which simply says that women shall have equal political rights with men. I have been told by one Senate staff member that it is very difficult politically for the Senate to vote on the Genocide Convention and a SALT treaty in the same year. That may seem hard to believe, but nevertheless I think it reflects the reality of the Senate. The Senate has very strong feelings about federal-state relationships; it has very strong feelings about legislating on domestic matters by way of treaty; and it has very strong feelings about what is a proper subject for the treaty power.

The human rights community sometimes has an unfortunate tendency to avoid talking to the Senate, and then it wonders why the Senate will not ratify the treaties. Work has got to be done in convincing the U.S. Senate, because that is now the key body in this operation. Mr. Hannum said that there was a missing speech here tonight—that there should have been a speech devoted to the proposition that given the reservations and understandings recommended by the administration, we should not ratify these treaties. I strongly disagree. I think the missing speech here is that we should not ratify the treaties at all, with or without any reservations. That might be the majority sentiment in the country. It has to be dealth with, and the question is how to best deal with it. Is it worth the reservations, understandings, and declarations? Are we getting ourselves into something that we would be better off not doing? I think that it certainly is desirable, even with the few reservations and understandings we have recommended, to subject the U.S. to international scrutiny, which these treaties do, and to make an international commitment along the lines set forth in the conventions. That is a substantial advance. It may not change U.S. law, but it would establish an international commitment to advanced human rights norms, and that impresses me as a worthwhile gain.

It may have been mentioned here that in fact there are no reservations, understandings, or declarations with respect to the vast bulk of the provisions of these four treaties. I think it was perhaps a bit unfair not to mention it, and I shall do so at this point. Further, nothing is set in concrete; each of the qualifications is subject to change.

It has been maintained that we have given away all of our bargaining chips, and that perhaps we could have come in later with these kinds of statements if necessary. But the process does not work that way. If we transmit to the Senate a treaty that has legal problems, we are much less likely to have it approved. In any event, we will be asked by the Senate what the problems are, and whether there are any clauses that require reservations, understandings, or declarations. It is not good enough to say that we have given away too much. It is inappropriate to do otherwise than to submit treaties on a basis upon which we can ratify them. This is not giving away bargaining chips; it is doing precisely what we would be asked to do in any event. Professor Henkin says that we will not be making any changes in U.S. law, and that we had written a reservation stating that there will be no changes in U.S. law, but we have not suggested a separate reservation stating that the treaties will only be ratified on the basis of compatibility with U.S. law.

Professor Henkin asked, "What if every country did this?" In fact, many countries have done exactly what we have done. Which countries? Those that take human rights seriously. It is very easy to sign a human rights treaty without any reservations or understandings. Many authoritarian regimes have done so. The liberal democracies have not taken that approach.

It is true that Canada became a party to the human rights covenants without any reservations, understandings, or declarations. Given the system in Canada, these treaties become internal Canadian law only if there is legislation enacted by the provinces. The Canadian government did not seek that legislation, and thus, the treaties are not internal law in Canada. There is an international commitment; Canada has become a party, but the Human Rights Covenants are not law within Canada. As you know, it is not legally possible for the U.S. to adopt that kind of approach. I think it would be profitable to examine how other liberal democracies have done it.

Finland has a string of seven reservations to the Covenant on Civil and Political Rights. Each of them is designed to make the covenants and Finnish law completely compatible. Finland has assumed that the way to approach this is to match Finnish law against the treaty provisions and, if there is a difference, to enact a reservation. For example, with respect to Article 9, paragraph 3, of the covenant, Finland declares that, according to the present Finnish legislation, the administrative authorities may take decisions concerning arrest or imprisonment, in which event the case is taken up for decision in court only after a certain time lapse. With respect to Article 10, paragraphs 2 and 3, Finland declares that although juvenile offenders are, as a rule, segregated from adults, this is not always deemed appropriate. There are seven straight references to Finnish legislation.

Denmark, while issuing a smaller number of such statements, has used the same approach. The United Kingdom—where, I might mention, every treaty is non-self-executing—has done the same thing. They have four important reservations that make British law and the convention compatible with each other. They have another string of reservations that has to do with application to territories. These are not really relevant for our purpose.

The point is that in many cases one can almost judge those nations that take human rights obligations seriously by the manner in which they have approached the problems of reservations or understandings to particular provisions. Italy has just become a party, and it has used reservations to make the treaties compatible with its law. Austria has just become a party and has done the same thing. It is instructive to look at the two Germanys. The Federal Republic has several statements, but East Germany has practically nothing. They have one short statement that all states have a right to become parties. I think that it is not exactly a close question as to who is being serious about their human rights obligations and who is not. If I had to choose, I would say that those Western liberal democracies that are entering a few reservations to make their law and the treaties compatible are doing a better job, a more serious

job, and a more committed job because they are taking
the treaties more seriously than those nations that become parties with no intention of conforming their
practices to their human rights treaty obligations and
that make no statements indicating that they have any
problems.

The notion of "non-self-executing" has been much
bandied about. The impression has been given that unless we enact legislation, the treaties will not be law in
the U.S. We do not need legislation for the vast bulk of
the provisions, if, indeed, we need it for any of the
provisions of these conventions. The law is already on
the books—in some cases we have had that law since
the beginning of the Republic.

It is true that if the treaties are not self-executing, the
courts will not apply them as such in any cases before
them. This is not to say that the courts can never examine the treaties insofar as they may provide assistance in interpreting a particular human rights provision,
or a civil rights provision, of U.S. law. However, the
courts will not apply the treaties directly as law.

This approach does not take the U.S. out of the main-
stream of the international protection of human rights.
The international commitment is still there, and there
are many other countries that, like Great Britain, do
not permit self-executing treaties. Great Britain will not
enter into a treaty unless the supporting legislation is
already extant or unless the government can get legislation to implement the treaty.

Professor Henkin said that we are expected to make
new law by treaty. That is perhaps the heart of the matter. Yes, we have very often made law, *new* law, by treaty.
We have overridden statutory law and prior treaties by
a new treaty. But we have not created new U.S. law by
treaty in the human rights area, and that is where we
really confront our basic problem with the U.S. Senate.
Many Senators feel very strongly (although the execu-

tive branch and the human rights community disagree just as strongly) that human rights is not a proper subject for the treaty power. They say that there are severe limits to the extent to which a nation can and should shape its domestic social, economic, and political order by making a treaty. Such matters can and should be dealt with by local communities, towns and cities, states, and even by the federal government. Other Senators do not object to an international commitment on human rights and a review of our practices by the international community, but shaping U.S. human rights law directly through a treaty on this subject goes beyond limits acceptable to them.

At a Senate hearing not very long ago, even genocide was perceived as an improper subject for the treaty power. A liberal Senator questioned us by saying, "Well, look, isn't genocide really murder after all, and isn't murder a crime within the jurisdiction of the states, and should the federal government be undertaking obligations at all in this area, let alone treaty obligations?" I think certain accommodations have got to be made to this kind of thinking.

I believe that if we were to take completely seriously the comments we have heard tonight, we will have two results.

1. The treaties will not be approved. They may not be anyway, but they would certainly be defeated with the approach that has been urged upon the government tonight.
2. We would have the Bricker Amendment all over again.

It has been suggested that that is an anachronism—the Bricker Amendment days are gone. But last year Representative John Ashbrook of Ohio introduced the Bricker Amendment again. Senator Fulbright said just a couple of years ago that the Bricker people were right. This is part of a larger movement, in terms of congressional-executive relationships, that is far from dead. The Dulles doctrine was effective in warding off the Bricker Amendment, but it was destructive for the human rights treaties. Yet we have been left with that legacy, and the connection between the two is very much alive. If we were going to enter into these kinds of treaties as the self-executing law of the land, we would have Bricker problems again, and difficult choices would then have to be made.

As far as the federal-state clause is concerned, I think it is clear that the vast majority of the article in these treaties are now within federal legislative or judicial jurisdiction, and in that sense the federal government has already undertaken responsibilities in these areas. There is very little in any of the conventions that is left to the states. A federal-state clause will not have much impact.

I will make one more plea to this group to take seriously the opposition to these treaties—opposition that is very real and very strong and that is focusing on issues not even mentioned tonight. The opposition is focusing on the loopholes in these treaties and on the UN enforcement system—which they perceive as biased against the West, and particularly the U.S. They are also saying that human rights is not a proper subject for the treaty power. The opposition is getting a response, of course.

It is also worth noting that the great majority of U.S. treaties sent to the Senate are approved by the Senate within two to six months from the time they are transmitted. Occasionally, Senate approval is quicker than that, and occasionally it takes longer. But so far the Genocide Convention has waited for almost thirty years. The Human Rights Covenants and the Racial Discrimination Convention were transmitted on February 23, 1978, and have thus already waited almost one year—well past the Senate average. There is no sign that anything will happen this year. We may have a hearing this year or we may not, according to the staff of the Senate Foreign Relations Committee. There will certainly be no Senate approval this year. There will be no Senate approval next year because it is a presidential election year. Perhaps 1981 is the first possible opening.

I believe it would be far more worthwhile for the human rights community to be working *with* the administration for the ratification of these treaties, even on the basis we have recommended. The treaties require the approval of a Senate that does not appear to be enthused about them. It is a cause of much regret to me that we have this difference with friends—personal friends and institutional friends. I think the differences should not be allowed to weaken the effort to ratify the treaties, and I hope and believe that we will find a way to reconcile our positions.

My basic plea to this group is to listen to and talk to the treaty opponents, and most importantly, to listen to and to talk to the members of the U.S. Senate, because they are the ones who need to be convinced and they are now the key to U.S. participation in the international human rights treaties.

JACK GOLDKLANG

*   *   *

Arthur Rovine has covered much of what we have to say. As a representative of the Department of Justice, I think I serve as a missing link. On the one hand, I have worked on the international aspects of human rights. I have been at the Human Rights Commission and at the Third Committee of the General Assembly, and I was on the team that negotiated the American Convention. I have gone through three sets of hearings on the Genocide Convention. At the same time, I have also worked on a day-to-day basis with the drafting of legislation and with trying to see how these rights are translated into our domestic law. It has been my experience, by and large, that the people who work in the international human rights field and the people who work in the domestic human rights field live in two different worlds and rarely communicate with each other. This is part of the problem that we have.

There is some symbolic value in holding this meeting here in a Senate hearing room. I hope that it is not only symbolic and that we get to hold some *real* hearings on these treaties. I fear that if we adopt the rather rigid approach suggested by the earlier speakers we may never get to do that; Amnesty International is obviously displeased with the approach taken in our messages transmitting the treaties to the Senate.

Our reason for not having become party to these treaties is not that we fear criticism in an international forum. After all, great debates at the UN on human rights already take place in the General Assembly, the Security Council, and the Human Rights Commission. We in this country have the give and take of an open society. Other countries read our newspapers and see exactly what is going on here. One of the nice things about being a member of the U.S. delegation to one of these bodies is that you do not have to get up and deny something that is going on at home. In contrast to the workings of the political organs of the UN, the proceedings that go on in the special committees created by these treaties are relatively discreet. Thus far, they have not been the scene of international embarrass-

ment for anybody. In fact, when you read the reports
that come out of some of these committees, it is somewhat difficult to find out what is going on.

I think that the real problem is the difficulty in meld-
ing these treaties with our own very complex domestic
legal system. I do not know how many of you in the
audience have actually sat down and tried to read
through the texts of all of these treaties. I found it fas-
cinating that on a panel filled with highly skilled lawyers, nobody pointed out an ambiguity or a possible
inconsistency with our domestic law that we had over-
looked in our messages to the Senate. I am sure, however, that if we have hearings before the Senate, we will
be met with dozens of such examples. They exist. In-
genious committee counsel could challenge us and
make us explain every last clause in these treaties.

We have heard a lot about the problem of treaties
that are self-executing. The administration took the
position that the substantive provisions of these treaties
should not be self-executing. In most cases, our substantive law incorporates the rights embodied in these
treaties. The treaty language, however, is often different from our own language. If these treaties were to
become laws of the U.S. directly enforceable in the
courts, *i.e.*, self-executing treaties, then we would have
a legal nightmare. First, we would have our state laws,
local laws, and federal laws. Second, the courts would
have to try to interpret how this other body of long and
complicated treaties fits in. If the treaties were law in
our own courts, we would have to be twice as careful in
drafting understandings and declarations and in clear-
ing up ambiguities.

We have the same obligation whether the treaties are
self-executing or not. We have an *international* obligation to have the proper laws and to live up to what we
promised in these treaties. The fact that we have recommended declarations to be adopted by the Senate

that these treaties are not self-executing does not change the situation. When these treaties were drafted, they were written so they would not be self-executing. They include statements that parties shall undertake to enact legislation to do certain things. It would be too complicated to analyze the treaties in detail here. I will take one single example—the American Convention on Human Rights. Article 2 discusses the method of implementation by domestic legislation. Our delegate, at the time the treaty was adopted, said:

> Some countries may choose to make the articles of the treaty effective *ipso facto* as domestic law and this article would permit them to do so. . . . Other states may prefer to rely solely on domestic law to implement the articles of the treaty. In the U.S. we would interpret this article as authorizing us to follow the last course in the case of the matters [dealing with] the substantive portions of the convention. That will permit us to apply, where appropriate, our Constitution, our domestic legislation, . . . in carrying out the obligations of the Convention. . . . In other words it is not the intention of the U.S. to interpret the articles . . . as being self-executing.[1]

No one at the conference objected to that position, because everybody realized that nations have to adopt treaties to their own legal systems. As Arthur Rovine said, some countries, such as the United Kingdom, have no self-executing treaties. The proposed declaration is designed, therefore, to clarify our position and to avoid litigation. But even without the declaration, the same result would be reached.

I do not believe that the substance of our reservations goes too far. There was a suggestion at one time that we simply have a blanket reservation saying "subject to the

1. 9 Int'l Legal Materials 715 (1970).

provisions of American law." Some people thought this would undermine the treaties because we would be limited simply to the status quo. I think that it would be a far better world if every nation simply pledged to observe its own laws scrupulously and if there were an enforceable mechanism to make sure they did. Often the worst, most despotic countries have beautiful-looking laws.

The administration has been attacked for proposing reservations to accommodate domestic law; I think this is a bit of a red herring. In some cases we have made reservations to avoid what might be very serious sideshows—by that I mean that some of the articles deal with things that are highly controversial as matter of domestic social and legal policy. For example, the American Convention provides for protecting life "from the moment of conception." (Article 4[1]). We have drafted a reservation for this article stating our adherence "is subject to the Constitution and other laws of the United States" because we would not want to divert the hearings into the side issue of the question of abortion.

Many countries, when they submit reports or reservations under these treaties, give themselves an *A*. They say, "Oh, yes, we have this; we have no problems." Because we take these things seriously, we did not give ourselves an *A*. We went through these treaties very carefully and tried to see exactly where we had legal problems. If, in the future, we amend our legislation, or if we have other reasons for doing so, we can always rescind a reservation. But we thought the present approach was a particularly good one. If we did not do this, we would have to reexamine each of the domestic issues (*e.g.*, the death penalty and free speech), and we would never get the treaties through.

Another example, that was mentioned earlier this evening by Professor Henkin, was the double jeopardy issue. We have proposed understandings on double jeopardy, consistent with Supreme Court decisions, so that a federal prosecution is not prohibited by an earlier state trial. The double jeopardy issue is a very important one to civil rights groups. When there is a civil rights violation committed and it appears that state officials have not prosecuted vigorously, they come to the Department of Justice and request our action. It is because we have this special federal-state rule on double jeopardy that we are able to provide that action. I do not want to get into an argument about the merits and demerits of this policy, but it is typical of the things that would become side issues in any hearing that we would have on the treaties if the reservations do not conform to American law.

I sincerely feel that the approach we have taken is a sensible one. Having appeared at hearings only last year on the Genocide Convention, I have seen that the things that some speakers claimed are obsolete, like states rights, are still very much alive. Although we are over on the far right on this particular panel, I think we represent the sensible middle course. If our friends who spoke earlier this evening testify that they prefer not to have the reservations that currently accompany the treaties, this is fine as long as they do not say we would rather not have the treaties at all. There is not just one, single way of drafting reservations. The proposed reservations were written over a long period of time by committee and by negotiation. We are always willing to consider constructive criticism. I have heard some particularly good examples at this conference. The basic approach we have taken is a sound one. I believe it will be our best hope of making some progress in getting the treaties approved.

DISCUSSION

* * *

Prof. Lillich: I would like to say two things at the outset. First of all, I think there is a consensus on the panel that we want these covenants ratified. The issue is how can we get the maximum amount of value out of these covenants for the U.S. both internationally and domestically. Second, with the exception of a few remarks by Lou Henkin and Art Rovine, we have not heard about what tactics we as a group can adopt in an attempt to get these covenants ratified. Art has suggested educating particular Senators in what is shaping up as a long ratification campaign. I would like to have some comments on this and other tactical suggestions. I think it may well be, given the tenor of Art's remarks, that this meeting will be the first of many meetings that the International Human Rights Law Group will have to hold on the ratification of these conventions. But if we have to come back here every year or so to remind the Senate and the Executive that we are here and that there is a human rights constituency out there, we will do it. Now, those prefatory remarks over, let us have the first speaker from the floor.

Prof. Elkind: I teach international law at the University of Auckland in New Zealand, where I have been working on problems involved in New Zealand's ratification of the covenants. May I say that I have made the assertion that the international covenants and the Racial Discrimination Convention are New Zealand's first and only Bill of Rights, and that I have been attempting to demonstrate to New Zealanders how these covenants may be invoked internationally in the defense of human rights. I hope now that you will permit me a few comments on the very peculiar assumptions upon which this ratification message and these reservations are based.

First, the letter of transmittal states that wherever a provision is in conflict with U.S. law, a reservation or understanding or declaration has been recommended. This strikes me as most peculiar, and in my opinion it is likely to strike the international community as most peculiar. It has always been my understanding that a state that ratifies a treaty intends to enter into certain legal obligations. My question is what legal obligation would the U.S. enter into by ratifying these covenants with these reservations? A non-self-executing human rights treaty hedged about by reservations designed to make the treaty entirely consistent with U.S. law is in fact no legal obligation at all. In the first place, let me question the constitutional authority to declare unilaterally that a treaty is non-self-executing. The question of whether a treaty is self-executing is, as you have pointed out, Mr. Rovine, entirely a question of internal constitutional law. As you've pointed out, in the U.K. *no* treaties are self-executing. Under the U.S. Constitution, however, there is a provision for the standing of treaties alongside U.S. law. My question is: are you not attempting to exclude the operation of Article VI of the U.S. Constitution by declaring the treaties to be non-self-executing, and if so can you do that?

Secondly, if we accept at face value your statements that the treaties are non-self-executing, then of course what we come to is something that is presumably addressed to the legislature. A treaty that is non-self-executing, as I understand it, is a call for law reform, for a change in legislation, to give better effect to human rights. But since you intend to make the treaties entirely consistent with U.S. law, what changes are you undertaking to make? What changes do you desire?

Finally, I have one more point, and that is that Canada has ratified the covenants with no reservations. Now Canada is a Commonwealth country. Its internal constitutional arrangements are such that *all* treaties are non-self-executing; consequently, you need provincial and dominion law in order to put them into effect. Canada, however, has not modified its international legal obligations, and reservations do go to international legal obligations. The U.S. reservations would be an attempt to modify the international legal obligations and would be seen as such. Consequently, I suggest that the counteroffer proposal that I heard is a very serious one. It is a question of good faith, and it may be seen as not being consistent with good faith—if, as I say, there is an attempt to enter into no legal obligation at all.

This problem is a serious one if you take a look at the reservations to Article 6 of the International Covenant of Civil and Political Rights. Now, as I recall, Article 6 is one of a number of provisions that, pursuant to Article 4, may not even be derogated from in times of national emergency. I would argue that they are fundamental provisions and that it is doubtful that you can have a reservation to such provisions.

Mr. Rovine: As far as non-self-execution is concerned, it does not mean that new legislation is required. It does mean that the treaty has got to be implemented by legislation, but if the legislation is already on the books, which in our case it is, then new legislation obviously is not required. These treaties are, it seems to us, on their face non-self-executing. Every one of them requires legislation or other measures to give them effect. That is not the language of a self-executing treaty, so that no matter what we said these would still be non-self-executing treaties as far as the courts of this country are concerned. It is true that it is a judicial doctrine, and you ask, what right do we have to say that they are non-self-executing—perhaps the assumption to the question being that it is a judicial doctrine and it's for the courts to determine it. Well, you are right, it is for the courts to determine it, but I think in light of the legislative history, which indicates they are non-self-executing, and in light of the language on the face of the documents, which indicates that they are non-self-executing, we wish to clear up any doubts about the question and to avoid litigation on the point by stating explicitly that they are non-self-executing. The courts are perfectly free to reject that view if they wish—I doubt they will. I think Jack has other points to make on the questions you have raised.

Mr. Goldklang: I don't think what we've done here is so unusual. I anticipated this comment and photocopied page 159 of Lou Henkin's book on *Foreign Affairs and the Constitution* (1972), where he says that on numerous occasions the Senate has provided by reservation that a treaty shall not take effect as domestic law but shall be implemented by Congress. Let me say that I don't think this is a reservation, because a reservation takes away from the force of the treaty, and all we are doing here is, I think, declaring what these treaties would be in any case, and the courts have always said that they will go by what the intent of the Executive was in becoming a party to the treaty. If you read the cases, they often seem rather annoyed in situations where they've been given no guidance. The typical case that gets into court is one where clearly the problem was not anticipated, and the court has to make a commonsense judgment as to whether something is specific enough to be enforced or whether it is not. Here, anticipating the wide across-the-board effect that this might have—and the opportunities for confusion in litigation that might be generated, as well as the chaos—we felt the responsible thing to do was to make this a declaration so that when it is published in our treaty series it will be available right along with the text of the treaty and one will not have to go back to statements made at the time of ratification.

Mr. Rovine: One quick point to illustrate the strength of feeling on this issue in the Senate: several years ago Senator Church, a liberal on the issue of human rights treaties and certainly on the Genocide Convention, came to the Department of State, and he said, "We hope you will not become a party to this convention, that you will not deposit the instrument of ratification [which is the last step needed to become a party], until the implementing legislation has been adopted." We assured him that that would be the case. He then asked for written assurance. The written assurance was given. He then came back and said, "Well, even the written assurance is not good enough, so we are going to tack on a little understanding by the Senate that the U.S. will not become a party to the Genocide Convention until the implementing legislation has been adopted." Now, this is an incredible response, because the Genocide Convention creates criminal offenses, and you cannot create criminal law in this country by way of treaty. You need implementing legislation. But Senator Church was so frightened of the thought that he tacked on this quite unnecessary understanding as to implementing legislation; and this response comes from a liberal. If you get such a response from liberal Senators on the Genocide Convention, I do not think it takes much imagination to guess what we are going to get on the treaties we are now discussing.

Member of Audience: I would like to address my question to both Prof. Elkind and the people who would prefer not to see the treaties ratified than to see them ratified with the reservations. How can you ask the U.S. to ratify a treaty that in Article 4 declares as an offense the dissemination of certain information and, at the same time, another treaty that declares that everyone shall have the right to freedom of expression, including the freedom to seek, receive, and impart information and ideas of all kind? You are asking the Senate to consent to both of those provisions without reservations.

Mr. Hannum: Too many people have dismissed the possibility of not ratifying the covenants with the present reservations, understandings, and so on. Given Mr. Rovine's prediction, which I am sure is correct, of the likelihood that these covenants will not even get a serious hearing in the Senate until 1981, I think that some alternative courses might be suggested, one of which would be for the administration simply to withdraw these covenants at this time from the Senate with the understanding that they would be resubmitted in several years, and to give the human rights community, which I agree does spend an awful lot of time talking with itself, a chance to talk to the administration. It is clear that they did not have that chance prior to the formulation of these messages. The outrage that the people on this panel have expressed did not come because they had long talks and did not get what they wanted. I think if this were done, if there were some further consultation within the administration and within human rights groups, then perhaps a much more united front could be presented to overcome what is assuredly a recalcitrant Senate. Perhaps we should think a little more imaginatively instead of feeling that all we have is the President's message.

Mr. Goldklang: It is not necessary to withdraw these in order to work further on the reservations. I have heard at least one useful suggestion tonight. I think it was said at one point that mentioning the Constitution is enough. You do not have to take constitutional law and practice and point out how this might be used perversely. Certainly fine tuning can be done on these, although what I think we are basically talking about is a difference in approach, which I understand, and which the Senate will understand, and which ultimately they will have to decide.

Prof. Lillich: You now have an opportunity to listen to the Senate via Mr. Tipson, who works for Senator Percy.

Mr. Tipson: Well, since you've said that, I had better issue a stronger than usual caveat. I work for Percy subject to the self-destruct clause—a one-year fellowship that has only six months to run [laughter].

But you invited us to talk strategy and I wanted to respond to that having had six months up here to become an expert on the Senate [laughter]. If there's one thing I have learned, it is that you cannot walk these things back. It seems to me that now the administration has sent these treaties over and made a commitment, a political commitment, that itself is a victory that must be taken advantage of. It would simply be a bad thing politically to suggest that we ought to try again some other time.

Second, and more fundamentally, it seems to me to be a serious problem to take the approach that these treaties, or any treaties, are somehow pure and should not be changed; that they should not be scrutinized carefully by the U.S. Indeed, the U.S. should *insist* on certain kinds of reservations flowing from its own experience in the human rights area, with the expectation that we have something to teach the rest of the world as well as something to learn in ratifying these agreements.

Third, it seems to me a fatal mistake to come on as though this is a liberal versus conservative issue: that the treaties represent the progressive wave of the future in the international community and the people that may oppose them are conservatives. This is wrong for more general reasons, but it is also wrong in terms of tactics, for in the last few years a number of conservatives have become strong advocates of human rights in certain contexts—the right to emigrate, the Helsinki Declaration—in ways that seem to me could be taken advantage of politically in trying to get these agreements accepted. If we come on as liberals pushing the liberal line in the world community, it will die like a duck. Moreover, it seems to me that that is not the case: there are some strong arguments pro and con for certain parts of these agreements—and the whole process of considering them ought to be a debate on the substance, rather than just a question of whether we are a progressive country or we are not a progressive country, which is the way the debate is in danger of becoming characterized.

Member of Audience: I just want to make one point that I always make to Jack Goldklang, and I have terrible trouble letting it go because I think it shows a failure to look at what is happening and what has happened in other places. And that relates to your argument that chaos is created or would be created if the treaties were not expressly declared to be non-self-executing. Have you any evidence? I tell you that you have not because I have made very extensive studies of Western European countries where these treaties are self-executing and where they have been applied in the courts, and they have not created any chaos. If you look, you would see, and they don't have to create chaos here. You have a lot of chaos because of various other laws.

Mr. Goldklang: I really think it is not worth discussing seriously.

Member of Audience: Let me make one other point, and that is that ever since the Bricker Amendment debate it has been said that the U.S. is the only country where treaties are self-executing. Many people believe that, and it is utterly false. Many countries, many Western countries—respected, progressive, and liberal countries—make their treaties self-executing. This is not something that we have to be afraid of. Let us argue the merits of particular issues—why this should be self-executing, why that should not be. But let us not, for heavens sake, look at these treaties and say *everything* in them should be non-self-executing.

Prof. Lillich: Any additional comments, statements of outrage, or concern?

Mr. Hawk: I have a comment, a suggestion, two concerns, and two questions. The comment is the note of disappointment in regard to the failure of this panel to address itself in any meaningful way to the Genocide Convention. I think that if any of these instruments gets to the floor of the Senate and generates a floor fight, that the spread of votes is probably not likely to be any more than six or seven, so that if you have to come back here next year and have another meeting like this to remind the Senate that they haven't held hearings or given their advice and consent to the four instruments you're talking about, I think you should also discuss the Genocide Convention.

The suggestion has to do with the reservations. I do not like them myself, in part because I don't understand them and moreover because I think that they are boring. But what I think you need to do is to move the issue of the reservations from the kind of adversarial proceedings now existing. My suggestion is that the administration appoint a lawyer and the nongovernmental organization (NGO) community hire another lawyer who would get together and try to work these things out and deal with some of the problems that the authors of the reservations were trying to get at without raising the problems that the law professors and the NGO world have pointed out.

My first concern is that I think there are a hundred people who work right around here who are able to introduce amendments deleting reservations. If there are Senators who can introduce amendments deleting reservations, I would suggest that people start now to try to find some Senators who will take offense at these reservations and who will move to delete them. What really concerns me is what certain other Senators will do to the treaties. I am very concerned that we will get some even more serious reservations coming out of the political process in the Senate.

My second concern is that you may be asking too much of the Civil and Political Covenant in regard to its applicability in domestic law. Ratification of the covenant does not stop Uruguay from torturing its citizens. At best, ratification of the covenant does stop some communities in Europe from a whole host of more minor violations of human rights. And I am not sure that you can ask a covenant to be a catchall for U.S. litigants.

I'd like to know if any of the panelists think that any of the obstacles to ratification are insurmountable, and I'd like to ask Professor Buergenthal how he thinks it will be possible to avoid infuriating the feminists and the anti-abortionists in implementing the American Convention?

Prof. Lillich: Let's start with the last question, as it will be the most difficult.

Prof. Buergenthal: I think on that problem the administration proposes each nation should take care of things itself. In effect, it leaves the issue where it finds it. And I must say that in this particular case I think that might not be a bad idea.

Mr. Hawk: Is there a consensus on the panel that that approach will actually work?

Mr. Rovine: I think that the approach has been well described by Professor Buergenthal. I think that is an apt description of it. Just leave the issue where it was. Abortion is an issue that the Senate, naturally, does not want to have to debate, and the difficulty, the real difficulty here, is that the provision is an illustration of the fact that not every clause in a human rights instrument is good simply because it's in a human rights instrument. Banning abortion is a very good example of a poor human rights clause. The Senate, not wanting to get involved in it, will probably just put the American Convention last on its list of human rights treaty priorities. I doubt that we are going to get any action from the Senate on that one for a long time to come. I did not say, incidentally, that there would not be a hearing until 1981—I said that there would not be any action until then.

Prof. Lillich: I'd like to sum up by relieving myself of a few of my frustrations generated by this evening's session. I must say I am somewhat saddened and disappointed—not of course by the performance of my colleagues on one side or the other—but by the somewhat limited focus I think we are taking on this issue. I think we can admit, as Burns Weston has said, that there certainly is a feeling in the international human rights community that there was not sufficient consultation with the prime constituency behind these treaties before the President's message came out. I think that was a devastating tactical error. I have mentioned it to Art before. I think other people in the government appreciate that now. However, that is water over the dam.

I also agree that these reservations and understandings are water over the dam. You cannot go back once you issue a message like the President's. As Fred Tipson said, you are not going to roll back the clock in this regard. Moreover, I don't think that you are going to find any Senators who are going to propose the elimination of any of these reservations. I think we are stuck. I think we are really going to have to come down eventually to the question proposed by Hurst Hannum, by Frank Newman, and by some others in the human rights community. Parenthetically, I was surprised to hear Lou raise this argument tonight, because he challenged Frank on that at the ABA's recent National Institute on International Human Rights Law. I think it will eventually come down, perhaps, not even to, Do we take them warts and all? but Do we take them with all these warts plus a lot of other things that may be tacked on as they sail through the Senate? Thus, I think we have got to take a lot of steps. One of the steps has been suggested by Art tonight. I really do believe that we have got to go out and talk to the Senators. I have been contacting one Senator on the Genocide Convention, intermittently, through a variety of people, for the last six weeks. I think we have really got to adopt the Bruno Bitker approach to getting these things ratified. It takes a lot of politicking; it takes a lot of buttonholing. By the way, the reason why we do not have the Genocide Convention on the agenda this evening was that we were focusing just upon the President's message. We had hoped to have Bruno talk from the floor about the need for the prompt ratification of the Genocide Convention.

Another suggestion was made by one member of the panel and many of you have heard me say this over and over again. It is almost impossible in many instances to get the civil rights people and the international human-rights people together. As a matter of fact, the International Human Rights Law Group will hold a conference soon with lawyers from the ACLU and other civil rights organizations in attendance where we shall try to devise some strategy not only in this area, but in some other areas where we can cooperate. People who are very prominent in the ACLU lack adequate knowledge of these treaties and their potential impact and, therefore, fail to support them as they should.

Finally, I would like to say that I am particularly depressed by what I view as a very timid, cautious, and fearful attitude about what the Senate may do. If one has to compromise, one has to compromise; but to anticipate compromises, and, in effect, to hand over the potential of victory or at least partial victory before even having begun the battle, is in my opinion very poor strategy indeed. The Genocide Convention was signed in 1948. We began our debates on civil rights bills in 1948 as well. If you look at the history of the civil rights movement, you find that a tremendous amount of effort went into that year after year. But these things were fought, and I think we're going to have to do the same thing here. As Lou mentioned in his opening remarks, the Civil and Political Covenant is what the American way of life is all about. This is the triumph of our values that we know very well we could not get through the present General Assembly; we could not get any kind of general consensus on it today. I think the same point was made by Clyde Ferguson tonight with respect to the Racial Discrimination Convention. We had a tremendous input in the drafting of that convention. Sure, it has some poor phrases. Sure, it has some bad clauses. We have added some reservations to it that I certainly will agree with on free-speech grounds, as I will agree with the reservation with respect to the right-to-life issue in the American Convention. Nevertheless, these treaties would still help us so much not only internationally, as our guest speaker from England pointed out, but domestically as well. To say that these treaties are non-self-executing, therefore, is going to result in foreclosing even the consideration of a constitutional argument to the contrary. We are not going to let the courts look at them and that seems to me to be terribly self-defeating.

Nevertheless, as I said before, I view this as water over the dam. What I think we are going to have to do after tonight's session is to go back, do our homework, regroup our forces, and I think we will be back here, if not next year, then the year after that. I hope that we have all your names and addresses. I hope that we can have you working for us here in Washington. And I hope that those of you who are representing nongovernmental organizations will go back and talk to your groups and let them know that there are a great many people concerned who are thinking about alternative tactics. There will be a published transcript of this session, and a variety of other papers will be published shortly that will offer alternatives to these particular reservations. Through various associations like the American Society of International Law, the ACLU, and others, we hope to be able to provide a wide smorgasboard of ideas when the Senate finally decides to consider these treaties. I am a bit disappointed that apparently there may not be hearings this year, but let us keep our fingers crossed. Let us work for the ratification of the Genocide Convention as well, and let us not forget that we are here to get these four treaties ratified. I think to do so we have all got to put our collective shoulders to the wheel. With that, I thank you for coming, I thank our panel for devoting their time and effort, and we hope to see you, if not next year, perhaps in 1981.

APPENDIX

*   *   *

Message from the
President of the United States
Transmitting Four Treaties
Pertaining to Human Rights

Senate Executives C, D, E, and F, 95th Congress, 2d
Session

*The International Convention on the Elimination of All Forms of
Racial Discrimination, signed on behalf of the United States on
September 28, 1966 (Executive C, 95–2); The International Covenant on Economic, Social and Cultural Rights, signed on behalf of
the United States on October 5, 1977 (Executive D, 95–2); The
International Covenant on Civil and Political Rights, signed on
behalf of the United States on October 5, 1977 (Executive E, 95–2);
and The American Convention on Human Rights, signed on behalf
of the United States on June 1, 1977 (Executive F, 95–2)*

February 23, 1978.—Treaties were read the first time and, together with the
accompanying papers, referred to the Committee on Foreign Relations and
ordered to be printed for the use of the Senate

LETTER OF TRANSMITTAL

THE WHITE HOUSE, *February 23, 1978.*

To the Senate of the United States:

With a view to receiving the advice and consent of the Senate to ratification, subject to certain reservations, understandings and declarations. I transmit herewith four treaties pertaining to human rights. Three of these treaties were negotiated at the United Nations:

—The International Convention on the Elimination of All Forms of Racial Discrimination, signed on behalf of the United States on September 28, 1966.

—The International Covenant on Economic, Social and Cultural Rights, signed on behalf of the United States on October 5, 1977.

—The International Covenant on Civil and Political Rights, signed on behalf of the United States on October 5, 1977.

The fourth treaty was adopted by the Organization of American States in 1969, and is open for adoption only by members of that Organization: The American Convention on Human Rights, signed on behalf of the United States on June 1, 1977.

I also transmit, for the information of the Senate, the report of the Department of State on the United Nations treaties and the Department's separate report on the American Convention.

While the United States is a leader in the realization and protection of human rights, it is one of the few large nations that has not become a party to the three United Nations human rights treaties. Our failure to become a party increasingly reflects upon our attainments, and prejudices United States participation in the development of the international law of human rights. The two human rights Covenants are based upon the Universal Declaration of Human Rights, in whose conception, formulation and adoption the United States played a central role. The Racial Discrimination Convention deals with a problem which in the past has been identified with the United States; ratification of this treaty will attest to our enormous progress in this field in recent decades and our commitment to ending racial discrimination.

The United States participated actively and effectively in the negotiation of the American Convention of Human Rights. That Convention, like the United Nations Covenant on Civil and Political Rights, treats in detail a wide range of civil and political rights. Freedom of speech and thought, participation in government, and others are included which Americans have always considered vital to a free, open and humane society. United States ratification of the Convention will give us a unique opportunity to express our support for the cause of human rights in the Americas.

The great majority of the substantive provisions of these four treaties are entirely consistent with the letter and spirit of the United States Constitution and laws. Wherever a provision is in conflict with United States law, a reservation, understanding or declaration has been recommended. The Department of Justice concurs in the judgment of the Department of State that, with the inclusion of these reservations, understandings and declarations, there are no constitutional or other legal obstacles to United States ratification. The reports of the Department of State on these four treaties describe their provisions and set forth the recommended reservations, understandings and declarations.

Should the Senate give its advice and consent to ratification of the Convention on the Elimination of All Forms of Racial Discrimination, I would then have the right to decide whether to make a declaration, pursuant to Article 14 of the Convention, recognizing the competence of the Committee on the Elimination of Racial Discrimination to receive and consider communications from individuals. Such a declaration would be submitted to the Senate for its advice and consent to ratification.

Should the Senate give its advice and consent to ratification of the International Covenant on Civil and Political Rights, I intend upon deposit of United States ratification to make a declaration, pursuant to Article 14 of the Covenant. By that declaration the United States would recognize the competence of the Human Rights Committee established by Article 28 to receive and consider "communications to the effect that a State Party claims that another State Party is not fulfilling its obligations under the Covenant."

Should the Senate give its advice and consent to ratification of the American Covention on Human Rights, I intend upon deposit of United States ratification to make a declaration pursuant to Article 45 of the Convention. By that declaration the United States would recognize the competence of the Inter-American Commission on Human Rights established by Article 33 to receive and examine "communications in which a State Party alleges that another State Party has committed a violation of a human right set forth in this Convention."

By giving its advice and consent to ratification of these treaties, the Senate will confirm our country's traditional commitment to the promotion and protection of human rights at home and abroad. I recommend that the Senate give prompt consideration to the treaties and advise and consent to their ratification.

JIMMY CARTER.

LETTER OF SUBMITTAL

DEPARTMENT OF STATE,
Washington, December 17, 1977.

The President,
The White House.

THE PRESIDENT: I have the honor to submit to you, with a view to their transmission to the Senate for advice and consent to ratification subject to specified reservations, understandings and declarations, three related treaties:

—The International Convention on the Elimination of All Forms of Racial Discrimination, adopted by the United Nations General Assembly on December 21, 1965.

—The International Covenant on Economic, Social and Cultural Rights, adopted by the United Nations General Assembly on December 16, 1966.

—The International Covenant on Civil and Political Rights, adopted by the United Nations General Assembly on December 16, 1966.

These treaties are designed to implement the human rights provisions of the Charter of the United Nations which, in Articles 1, 55 and 56, provides that the Organization and its members shall promote "universal respect for, and observance of, human rights and fundamental freedoms for all without distinction as to race, sex, language, or religion."

The Convention on the Elimination of all Forms of Racial Discrimination and the two Human Rights Covenants together constitute a paramount contribution to the development of the international law of human rights. The Convention on Racial Discrimination and the Covenant on Civil and Political Rights are in the legal and ethical tradition of the West. They give expression to human rights that are, for the most part, accepted in United States law and practice. The Covenant on Economic, Social and Cultural Rights while also reflective of United States law and policy, is primarily a statement of goals to be achieved progressively, rather than through immediate implementation.

The three treaties have been widely approved by the world community. The Convention on Racial Discrimination, which entered into force January 4, 1969, now numbers 98 countries among its parties; the Covenant on Economic, Social and Cultural Rights, which entered into force January 3, 1976, has 46 ratifications or accessions, and the Covenant on Civil and Political Rights, which entered into force March 23, 1976, has 43 ratifications or accessions. It is increasingly anomalous that the list of parties does not include the United States, whose human rights record domestically and internationally has long served as an example to the world community. The Covenants were signed for the United States on October 5, 1977; the Convention on Racial Discrimination was signed on September 28, 1966.

In view of the large number of States concerned and the disparity of view on some questions, it was not possible to negotiate treaties which were in perfect accord with the United States Constitution and law. The treaties contain a small number of provisions which are or appear to be in conflict with United States law. The most serious examples are paragraphs (a) and (b) of Article 4 of the Convention on Racial Discrimination, and Article 20 of the Covenant on Civil and Political Rights, which conflict with the right of free speech as protected by the Constitution. Reservations to these and other provisions, discussed below, along with a number of statements of understanding, are designed to harmonize the treaties with existing provisions of domestic law. In addition, declarations that the treaties are not self-executing are recommended. With such declarations, the substantive provisions of the treaties would not of themselves become effective as domestic law. The Department of Justice is of the view that, with these reservations, declarations and understandings, there are no constitutional or other legal objections to United States ratification of the treaties.

The following is a summary of the provisions of the terms of the treaties, and the reservations, declarations and understandings to them recommended to the Senate by the Departments of State and Justice.

*Convention on the Elimination of All Forms of Racial
Discrimination*

The Convention is designed to forbid racial and ethnic discrimination in all fields of public life. For the most part, its terms closely parallel United States constitutional and statutory law and policy. The Convention is divided into three parts: Part I (Articles 1 through 7) contains the substantive provisions; Part II (Articles 8 through 16) contains administrative and enforcement clauses; Part III (Articles 17 through 25) sets forth the final clauses.

Article 1 defines "racial discrimination" broadly, but specifies that the Convention does not apply to distinctions, exclusions, restrictions or preferences made by a State Party between citizens and non-citizens. Paragraph (4) of Article 1 and paragraph (2) of Article 2 also permit, but do not require, what have come to be known in the United States as "affirmative action" programs.

Article 2 specifies steps to be taken to eliminate racial discrimination, including nullification of discriminatory laws at all levels of political organization and prohibition of racial discrimination by "any persons, group or organization." Article 3 condemns and prohibits racial segregation and apartheid. These provisions, along with those of Article 5, require equality in several areas of economic, social and cultural rights, and the right of access to public places. They require a statement preserving United States distinctions between various governmental and private activities. The following understanding is recommended:

"The United States understands its obligation to exact legislation and take other measures under paragraph (1) of Article 2, subparagraphs (1)(c) and (1)(d) of Article 2, Article 3, and Article 5 to extend only to governmental or government-assisted activities and to private activities required to be available on a non-discriminatory basis as defined by the Constitution and laws of the United States."

Article 4 condemns propaganda and organizations based on racial hatred or superiority. Paragraph (c) of Article 4 requires that States Parties forbid public authorities or institutions, national or local, from promoting or inciting racial discrimination. This obligation is consonant with United States law and policy. Paragraphs (a) and (b), however, provide for restrictions on the dissemination of ideas, or participation in organizations based on those ideas, and as such would clearly violate the freedom of expression and association guaranteed by the Constitution and United States law and practice. With respect to paragraphs (a) and (b) of Article 4, the following reservation is recommended:

"The Constitution of the United States and Article 5 of this Convention contain provisions for the protection of individual rights, including the right to free speech, and nothing in this Convention shall be deemed to require or to authorize legislation or other action by the United States which would restrict the right of free speech protected by the Constitution, laws, and practice of the United States."

Article 5 enumerates certain fundamental rights the enjoyment and exercise of which must be protected against abridgement by racial discrimination. These rights include the basic civil and political rights guaranteed in the United States, such as rights to personal security, universal suffrage, freedom of movement, and freedom of thought and expression. The rights also include economic, social and cultural rights, including the right to form and join trade unions, the right to housing, the right to employment, and the right of access to any place or service intended for use by the general public. The obligation assumed under Article 5 is not designated primarily to protect or guarantee the several enumerated rights as such, but rather to assure equality and non-discrimination in the enjoyment of those rights.

Article 6 requires the provision of effective protection and remedies, through the competent tribunals and other government institutions, against acts of racial discrimination which violate the Convention. Article 7 commits States Parties to undertake active programs to combat racial discrimination and prejudice.

Articles 8 through 16 constitute the administrative and enforcement provisions of the Convention. A Committee on the Elimination of Racial Discrimination is established, along with a requirement that States Parties submit reports to the United Nations Secretary-General, for consideration by the Committee, describing the measures they have adopted which give effect to the provisions of the Convention. The Committee may make recommendations based on the reports and information received from States Parties.

A procedure is also established permitting States Parties to submit complaints to the Committee alleging that other States Parties are not giving effect to the provisions of the Convention. A conciliation procedure constitutes the central mechanism for settling such disputes. No legally binding recommendations or awards are permitted.

Article 14 permits, but does not require, a State Party to declare that it recognizes the competence of the Committee to receive and consider communications from individuals or groups of individuals, within the jurisdiction of that State Party, claiming to be victims of a violation by that State Party of any of the rights set forth in the Convention. Individual complaints may be considered by the Committee only after all available domestic remedies have been exhausted.

Article 15 provides for the consideration by the Committee of reports on implementation of the Convention by States Parties in non-self-governing territories over which they exercise jurisdiction.

Article 16 confirms that the procedures for resolution of disputes and complaints provided in the Convention are additional to rather than substitutes for other procedures agreed to by the States Parties.

Articles 17 through 25 are the final clauses. Article 22 provides that any dispute with respect to the interpretation or application of the Convention which is not settled by negotiation or by the procedures provided for in the Convention shall at the request of any party to the dispute be referred to the International Court of Justice unless the disputants agree to another mode of settlement.

In addition to the general understanding and reservation recommended above, the following reservation is recommended:

"The United States shall implement all the provisions of the Convention over whose subject matter the Federal Government exercises legislative and judicial administration; with respect to the provisions over whose subject matter constituent units exercise jurisdiction, the Federal Government shall take appropriate measures, to the end that the competent authorities of the constituent units may take appropriate measures for the fulfillment of this Covenant."

This reservation is designed to deal with a number of provisions, notably subparagraphs (1)(a) and (1)(c) of Article 2, paragraph (c) of Article 4, Article 6, and Article 7, which impose obligations whose fulfillment is dependent upon the legal power of state and local governments as well as that of the Federal Government.

It is further recommended that a declaration indicate the non-self-executing nature of Articles 1 through 7 of the Convention. Absent such a statement, the terms of the Convention might be considered as directly enforceable law on a par with Congressional statutes. While the terms of the Convention, with the suggested reservations and understanding, are consonant with United States law, it is nevertheless preferable to leave any further implementation that may be desired to the domestic legislative and judicial process. The following declaration is recommended:

"The United States declares that the provisions of Articles 1 through 7 of this Convention are not self-executing."

International Covenant on Economic, Social and Cultural Rights

The International Covenant on Economic, Social and Cultural Rights sets forth a number of rights which, while for the most part in accord with United States law and practice, are nevertheless formulated as statements of goals to be achieved progressively rather than implemented immediately.

Parts I, II, and III of the Covenant (Articles 1 through 15) contain the substantive provisions; Part IV (Articles 16 through 23) sets forth the administrative provisions; and Part V (Articles 26 through 31) contains the final clauses.

Article 1 affirms in general terms the right of all peoples to self-determination, and the right to freely dispose of their natural wealth and resources without prejudice to any obligations arising out of international economic cooperation, based upon the principle of mutual benefit, and international law. This is consonant with United States policy.

Paragraph (1) of Article 2 sets forth the basic obligation of States Parties "to take steps," individually and through international assistance and cooperation, "to the maximum of its available resources, with a view to achieving progressively the full realization of the rights recognized" by the Covenant "by all appropriate means, including legislative measures." In view of the terms of paragraph (1) of Article 2, and the nature of the rights set forth in Articles 1 through 15 of the Covenant, the following statement is recommended:

"The United States understands paragraph (1) of Article 2 as establishing that the provisions of Articles 1 through 15 of this Covenant describe goals to be achieved progressively rather than through immediate implementation."

It is also understood that paragraph (1) of Article 2, as well as Article 11, which calls for States Parties to take steps individually and through international cooperation to guard against hunger, import no legally binding obligation to provide aid to foreign countries.

Paragraph (2) of Article 2 forbids discrimination of any sort based on race, color, sex, language, religion, political or other opinion, national or social origin, property, birth or other status. United States and international law permit certain limited discrimination against non-nationals in appropriate cases (*e.g.*, ownership of land or of means of communication). It is understood that this paragraph also permits reasonable distinctions based on citizenship. Paragraph (3) of Article 2 provides that developing countries, with due regard to human rights and their national economy, may determine to what extent they will guarantee the economic rights recognized in the Covenant to non-nationals. Of related significance is Article 25, which provides that nothing in the Covenant is to be interpreted as impairing the "inherent right of all peoples to enjoy and utilize fully and freely their natural wealth and resources." With respect to paragraph (3) of Article 2 and to Article 25, the following declaration is recommended:

"The United States declares that nothing in the Covenant derogates from the equal obligation of all States to fulfill their responsibilities under international law. The United States understands that under the Covenant everyone has the right to own property alone as well as in association with others, and that no one shall be arbitrarily deprived of his property."

This declaration and understanding will make clear the United States position regarding property rights, and expresses the view of the United States that discrimination by developing countries against nonnationals or actions affecting their property or contractual rights may only be carried out in accordance with the governing rules of international law. Under international law, any taking of private property must be nondiscriminatory and for a public purpose, and must be accompanied by prompt, adequate, and effective compensation.

Article 3 provides that the Parties undertake to ensure the equal rights of men and women with respect to the rights set forth in the Covenant. Article 4 permits derogation from the rights enumerated in the Covenant only by law for the general welfare and only insofar as such limitations may be compatible with the nature of the rights.

Paragraph (1) of Article 5 provides that nothing in the Covenant may be interpreted as implying for any State, group or person any right to engage in any activity or to perform any act aimed at the destruction of any of the rights or freedoms recognized in the Covenant, or at their limitation to a greater extent than provided for in the Covenant. This clause raises in indirect fashion the problem of freedom of speech, and accordingly, the following statement is recommended:

"The Constitution of the United States and Article 19 of the International Covenant on Civil and Political Rights contain provisions for the protection of individual rights, including the right to free speech, and nothing in this Covenant shall be deemed to require or to authorize legislation or other action by the United States which would restrict the right of free speech protected by the Constitution, laws, and practice of the United States."

Paragraph (2) of Article 5 provides that existing rights may not be restricted because they are not recognized in the Covenant or recognized to a lesser extent.

Articles 6 through 9 of the Covenant list certain economic

rights, including the right to work (Article 6), to favorable working conditions (Article 7), to organize unions (Article 8), and to social security (Article 9). Some of the standards established under these articles may not readily be translated into legally enforceable rights, while others are in accord with United States policy, but have not yet been fully achieved. It is accordingly important to make clear that these provisions are understood to be goals whose realization will be sought rather than obligations requiring immediate implementation.

Similarly, Articles 10 through 14 detail certain social rights, among them the right to protection of the family, including standards for maternity leave (Article 10), the right of freedom from hunger (Article 11), the right to physical and mental health (Article 12), and the right to education (Articles 13 and 14).Article 15 provides for certain cultural rights, all of which are appropriately protected by United States law and policy.

Articles 16 through 23 contain administrative provisions requiring the submission of reports on implementation of the Covenant to the United Nations Secretary-General for transmission to and consideration by the Economic and Social Council. The Council may transmit information and make recommendations.

Articles 26 through 31 are the final clauses. Article 28 states that "The provisions of the present Covenant shall extend to all parts of federal States without any limitations or exceptions." In view of the nature of the United States federal system, this Article is not acceptable as formulated. With respect to Article 28, the following reservation is recommended:

"The United States shall progressively implement all the provisions of the Covenant over whose subject matter the federal Government exercises legislative and judicial jurisdiction; with respect to the provisions over whose subject matter constituent units exercise jurisdiction, the Federal Government shall take appropriate measures, to the end that the competent authorities of the constituent units may take appropriate measures for the fulfillment of this Covenant."

In addition, it is further recommended that a declaration indicate the non-self-executing nature of Articles 1 through 15 of the Covenant. For the same reasons as set forth above with regard to the Convention on the Elimination of All Forms of Racial Discrimination, the following declaration is recommended:

"The United States declares that the provisions of Articles 1 through 15 of this Covenant are not self-executing."

International Covenant on Civil and Political Rights

The International Covenant on Civil and Political Rights is, of the three treaties submitted, the most similar in conception to the United States Constitution and Bill of Rights. The rights guaranteed are those civil and political rights with which the United States and the western liberal democratic tradition have always been associated. The rights are primarily limitations upon the power of the State to impose its will upon the people under its jurisdiction.

Parts I, II, and III of the Covenant (Articles 1 through 27) contain the substantive provisions; Part IV (Articles 28 through 45) contains the administrative and enforcement provisions; Part V includes under Articles 46 and 47 further substantive clauses; and Part VI (Articles 48 through 53) sets forth the final clauses.

Article 1, which contains provisions regarding self-determination and the right to dispose of natural wealth and resources, subject to the principles of mutual benefit and international law, is identical to Article 1 of the Covenant on Economic, Social and Cultural Rights.

Article 2 commits States Parties to provide the rights enumerated in the Covenant without regard to race, color, sex, language, religion, political or other opinion, national or social origin, property, birth or other status. States Parties are required to provide effective legal remedies for violations of the rights protected by the Covenant.

Article 3 expressly obligates States Parties to undertake to ensure the equal right of men and women to the enjoyment of the civil and political rights set forth in the Covenant.

Article 4 permits derogation from certain of the rights guaranteed by the Covenant in situations of public emer-

gency "which threatens the life of the nation" and the existence of which is officially proclaimed, provided that those
rights are not abridged on a discriminatory basis.

Paragraph (1) of Article 5 of the Covenant is identical to
paragraph (1) of Article 5 of the Covenant on Economic,
Social and Cultural Rights, and thus indirectly raises the
question of free speech. Article 20 expressly prohibits "any
propaganda for war" and "any advocacy of national, racial
or religious hatred that constitutes incitement to discrimination, hostility or violence." This provision conflicts with the
Constitution, and thus a reservation is required. Article 20
also appears to restrict the freedom of expression provided
for in Article 19 of the Covenant. With respect to Article 20
and to paragraph (1) of Article 5, the following reservation
is recommended:

"The Constitution of the United States and Article 19 of
this Covenant contain provisions for the protection of individual rights, including the right of free speech, and nothing
in this Covenant shall be deemed to require or to authorize
legislation or other action by the United States which would
restrict the right of free speech protected by the Constitution, laws, and practice of the United States."

Article 6 of the Covenant provides a general right to protection of life, and limits the circumstances in which capital
punishment may be imposed or carried out. Paragraph 2
indicates that the death sentence may be imposed only for
"the most serious crimes in accordance with law in force at
the time of the commission of the crime," and only pursuant
to a final judgment of a competent court. Paragraph 4 provides a right to seek pardon or commutation of the death
sentence. Paragraph 5 forbids execution of persons under
the age of 18 or of pregnant women. As United States law is
not entirely in accord with these standards, the following
reservation is recommended:

"The United States reserves the right to impose capital
punishment on any person duly convicted under existing or
future laws permitting the imposition of capital punishment."

Article 7 forbids torture and inhuman or degrading treatment or punishment. Article 8 forbids slavery.

Article 9 protects the right to liberty and security of the

person, and sets forth the conditions under which persons may be arrested and tried for criminal charges. Paragraph 5 grants a right to compensation for unlawful arrest or detention which goes beyond current federal law. A related provision is paragraph (1) of Article 15, which forbids ex post facto criminal offenses. The third clause of that paragraph provides that if, subsequent, to the commission of an offense, provision is made by law for the imposition of a lighter penalty, the offender is to benefit thereby. This right is often granted in practice in the United States, but is not required by law. With respect to paragraph (5) of Article 9 and to paragraph (1) of Article 15, the following reservation accordingly is recommended:

"The United States does not adhere to paragraph (5) of Article 9 or to the third clause of paragraph (1) of Article 15."

Article 10 establishes standards for the treatment of prisoners. Subparagraph (2)(a) of Article 10 requires that accused persons be segregated from convicted persons save in exceptional circumstances, while subparagraph (2)(b) requires that accused juvenile persons be separated from adults and brought as speedily as possible for adjudication. Paragraph (3) of Article 10 provides that the penitentiary system is to "comprise treatment of prisoners the essential aim of which shall be their reformation and social rehabilitation." Practice and policy in United States prisons does not fully accord with these standards, and accordingly, with respect to paragraphs (2) and (3) of Article 10, the following statement is recommended:

"The United States considers the rights enumerated in paragraphs (2) and (3) of Article 10 as goals to be achieved progressively rather than through immediate implementation."

Article 11 prohibits imprisonment solely on the basis of inability to fulfill a contractual obligation.

Article 12 guarantees the rights of freedom of movement and residence, and of emigration, to all those lawfully within the territory of a State Party. Article 13 permits aliens lawfully within the territory of a State Party to be expelled only in pursuance of a decision reached in accordance with law.

Article 14 establishes standards for the conduct of trials,

including the right to be presumed innocent. Paragraph (3) protects a defendant's right to counsel, including court-appointed counsel, to a speedy trial, to be informed of the charges against him, to subpoena and examine witnesses, and not to testify against himself. Paragraph (4) requires that juvenile courts "take account" of the age and possible rehabilitation of juvenile defendants. Paragraph (5) protects the right to appeal convictions. Paragraph (6) gives a right to compensation for miscarriage of justice under certain circumstances; this right is protected by the United States Code, Title 28, § 1495 and 2513. Paragraph (7) forbids re-trial for the same offence, following final conviction or acquittal for that offence.

It is possible to read all the requirements contained in Article 14 as consistent with United States law, policy and practice. However, the Senate may wish to record its understanding of certain provisions of that Article as follows:

"The United States understands that subparagraphs (3)(b) and (d) of Article 14 do not require the provision of court-appointed counsel when the defendant is financially able to retain counsel or for petty offenses for which imprisonment will not be imposed. The United States further understands that paragraph (3)(e) does not forbid requiring an indigent defendant to make a showing that the witness is necessary for his attendance to be compelled by the court. The United States considers that provisions of United States law currently in force constitute compliance with paragraph (6). The United States understands that the prohibition on double jeopardy contained in paragraph (7) is applicable only when the judgment of acquittal has been rendered by a court of the same governmental unit, whether the Federal Government or a constituent unit, which is seeking a new trial for the same cause."

Article 16 guarantees the right to recognition as a person before the law. Article 17 protects against interference with individual privacy.

Article 18 sets forth the right of freedom of thought, conscience and religion.

Other key rights provided for in the Covenant are those of peaceful assembly (Article 21), freedom of association

(Article 22), protection of the family, including the obligation of States Parties to take appropriate steps to ensure equality of rights and responsibilities between spouses (Article 23), protection of children without regard to their status at birth (Article 24), and participation in public's affairs, including voting and accession to public service (Article 25). Paragraph (b) of Article 25 provides that every citizen shall have the right and opportunity: "To vote and to be elected at genuine periodic elections which shall be by universal and equal suffrage and shall be held by secret ballot, guaranteeing the free expression of the will of the electors."

Article 26 provides that all persons are equal before the law and entitled to its equal protection, and generally prohibits discrimination.

Article 27 provides that in States in which ethnic, religious or linguistic minorities exist, persons belonging to such minorities are not to be denied the right, in community with other members of their group, to enjoy their own culture, to profess and practice their own religion, or to use their own language.

Part IV of the Covenant contains the administrative and enforcement provisions. A Human Rights Committee is established, and rules for its constitution and functioning are provided. The States Parties to the Covenant are required to submit reports to the United Nations Secretary-General for transmission to and consideration by the Committee, which may make findings and recommendations on the basis of the reports.

Article 41 permits, but does not require, a State Party to declare that it recognizes the competence of the Committee to receive and consider communications "to the effect that a State Party claims that another State Party is not fulfilling its obligations under the Covenant." If the Committee is unable to resolve a matter submitted to it pursuant to Article 41, a Conciliation Commission may be appointed, with the prior consent of the parties concerned. The good offices of the Commission are to be made available to the parties, and recommendations may be made by the Commission if a solution to the dispute is not reached.

Should the Senate give its advice and consent to ratification of the Covenant, it is contemplated that the United States will make a declaration pursuant to Article 41. It is in the interest of the United States to participate in and influence the State-to-State complaint procedure established by the Covenant, not least because it is to be hoped that the work of the Committee will contribute to the development of a generally accepted international law of human rights. It should be noted that declarations made pursuant to Article 41 may be withdrawn at any time by notification to the Secretary-General.

Part V of the Covenant contains two substantive provisions, Articles 46 and 47. Article 46 states that the Covenant is not to be interpreted as impairing the provisions of the United Nations Charter and of the constitutions of the specialized agencies which define the respective responsibilities of the various United Nations organs and of the agencies with respect to the matters dealt with in the Covenant.

Article 47 is identical to Article 25 of the Covenant on Economic, Social and Cultural Rights. It provides that nothing in the Covenant is to be interpreted as impairing the "inherent right of all peoples to enjoy and utilize fully and freely their natural wealth and resources." With respect to Article 47, the following declaration is recommended:

"The United States declares that the right referred to in Article 47 may be exercised only in accordance with international law."

Part VI of the Covenant (Articles 48 through 53) contains the final clauses. Article 50, which is identical to Article 28 of the Covenant on Economic, Social and Cultural Rights, explicitly requires that the Covenant be applied to all parts of federal States without limitation or exception. For the reasons set forth above regarding Article 28 of the Covenant on Economic, Social and Cultural Rights, the following reservation is recommended with respect to Article 50:

"The United States shall implement all the provisions of the Covenant over whose subject matter the Federal Government exercises legislative and judicial jurisdiction; with respect to the provisions over whose subject matter constituent units exercise jurisdiction, the Federal Government shall take appropriate measures, to the end that the competent authorities of the constituent units may take appropriate measures for the fulfillment of this Covenant."

In addition, it is further recommended that a declaration indicate the non-self-executing nature of Articles 1 through 27 of the Covenant. For the same reasons as set forth above with regard to the Convention on Racial Discrimination and the Covenant on Economic, Social and Cultural Rights, the following declaration is recommended:

"The United States declares that the provisions of Articles 1 through 27 of the Covenant are not self-executing."

A related instrument of significance which is not being submitted to the Senate at this time is the Optional Protocol to the International Covenant on Civil and Political Rights. The Optional Protocol, like Article 14 of the Convention on Racial Discrimination, establishes a procedure under which individuals who consider their rights under the Covenant to have been violated may, after exhausting all available domestic remedies, appeal in their individual capacity to the Human Rights Committee established by Article 28 of the Covenant. Any State that becomes a party to the Optional Protocol recognizes, by becoming a party, the competence of the Committee to receive and consider communications from individuals subject to the jurisdiction of that State who claim to be victims of a violation by that State of any of the rights set forth in the Covenant.

The Department of State believes that the three human rights treaties submitted with this report are now and will continue to be of cardinal importance in the progressive development of the international law of human rights. United States adherence to these treaties is in the national interest and in the interest of the world community. It is our hope that the United States, after the fullest consideration by the Senate, will become party to all three treaties.

Respectfully submitted.

WARREN CHRISTOPHER.

DEPARTMENT OF STATE,
Washington, December 17, 1977.

The PRESIDENT,
The White House.

THE PRESIDENT: I have the honor to submit to you, with a view to its transmission to the Senate for advice and consent to ratification subject to specified reservations, understandings and declarations, the American Convention on Human Rights, signed by you and by Ambassador Gale McGee on June 1, 1977. The Convention was negotiated at San Jose, Costa Rica in 1969 by the members of the Organization of American States with the active participation of the United States. It has been ratified or adhered to by Colombia, Costa Rica, Haiti, Honduras, and Venezuela. Entry into force of the Convention requires eleven ratifications or adherences by member States of the Organization of American States.

Along with the United Nations Covenants on Human Rights and the United Nations Convention on the Elimination of All Forms of Racial Discrimination, the American Convention on Human Rights constitutes a significant contribution to the developing international law of human rights. The American Convention, like the United Nations treaties, gives legally binding expression to human rights that are, for the most part, accepted in United States law and practice. The Convention provides for extensive protection of personal liberty, preserves the right to a fair trial, to freedom of assembly, and to participation in government, and protects many other rights of great significance to Americans. In addition, the Convention includes provisions which recognize certain rights that are not protected by the United Nations human rights treaties. Among the most important of these are the provision protecting the right to privacy (Article 11), and the provision concerning territorial application (Article 28), which takes account of the federal structure of many countries in the Western Hemisphere, including the United States.

The large number of States concerned and the disparity of views on certain questions made it impossible to negotiate a convention that was in every respect consonant with United

104

States law. The small number of provisions not in accord with United States law require reservations which, along with a number of interpretive understandings and declarations, will permit United States ratification of the Convention should the Senate give its approval. The Department of Justice is of the view that, with the reservations, understandings and declarations recommended below, there are no constitutional or other legal objections to United States ratification of the Convention.

The following is a summary of the provisions of the Convention, with the reservations, understandings and declarations to them recommended to the Senate by the Department of State.

The Convention begins with a general provision on non-discrimination (Article 1), and follows with an obligation to adopt legislative or other measures as may be necessary to give effect to the rights and freedoms protected by the Convention (Article 2). While the latter provision thus indicates that the substantive provisions of the Convention are not self-executing, in order to avoid possible discrepancies in wording and to leave the implementation of all substantive provisions to the domestic legislative and judicial process, the following declaration is recommended:

"The United States declares that the provisions of Articles 1 through 32 of this Convention are not self-executing."

This declaration will ensure that no substantive provisions of the Convention will operate as domestic law except insofar as they may be reflected in existing law or future legislation.

Articles 3 through 25 of the Convention set forth the fundamental civil and political rights protected by the Convention. Article 3, on juridical personality, states that every person has the right to recognition as a person before the law. Article 4 deals with the right to life generally, and includes provisions on capital punishment. Many of the provisions of Article 4 are not in accord with United States law and policy, or deal with matters in which the law is unsettled. The Senate may wish to enter a reservation as follows:

"United States adherence to Article 4 is subject to the Constitution and other law of the United States."

Article 5, on the right to humane treatment, bans cruel,

inhuman or degrading punishment, and requires that persons deprived of their liberty be treated with respect for the dignity of the human person.

Paragraph (4) of Article 5 provides that accused persons, except in unusual circumstances, are to be segregated from convicted persons. Paragraph (5) requires that minors subject to criminal proceedings are to be separated from adults and brought before specialized tribunals as speedily as possible. Paragraph (6) stipulates that punishment consisting of deprivation of liberty shall have as an essential aim the reform and social readaptation of prisoners.

Paragraphs (4) and (6) of Article 5 set forth standards of treatment for prisoners not yet met in United States practice. With respect to paragraph (5), the law reserves the right to try minors as adults in certain cases and there is no present intent to revise these laws. The following statement is recommended:

"The United States considers the provisions of paragraphs (4) and (6) of Article 5 as goals to be achieved progressively rather than through immediate implementation, and, with respect to paragraph (5), reserves the right in appropriate cases to subject minors to procedures and penalties applicable to adults."

Article 6, on freedom from slavery, prohibits all forms of involuntary servitude and compulsory labor. Paragraphs (2) and (3) expressly exempt from this prohibition forced labor in connection with a deprivation of liberty as punishment for certain crimes. Compulsory labor is also defined to exclude military service and service exacted in time of danger or calamity "that threatens the existence or well-being of the community."

Article 7, on the right to personal liberty, bars arbitrary arrest or imprisonment. Any person detained is to be informed of the reasons for his detention and promptly notified of any charges against him. Trial must be within "a reasonable time", with recourse to a competent court to decide on the lawfulness of the arrest or detention. Paragraph (7) provides that no one is to be detained for debt. This principle, however, is not to "limit the orders of a competent judicial authority issued for nonfulfillment of duties of support." The Senate may wish to record its understanding that the second sentence of paragraph (7) of Article 7 applies to orders of any competent judicial authority, whether or not issued for fulfillment of duties of support.

Article 8 sets forth the several procedural and other requirements necessary for a fair trial, including an independent and impartial tribunal, a presumption of innocence, language assistance if necessary, prior notification in detail of charges, adequate time and means for the preparation of a defense, the right to counsel of the defendant's own choosing, the right to counsel provided by the State, the right to examine witnesses in court and to obtain their appearance, the right not to be compelled to be a witness against oneself, and the right of appeal. Confessions of guilt are valid only if made without coercion of any kind. A statement of understanding is recommended as follows:

"The United States understands that subparagraph (2)(e) of Article 8 does not require the provision of court-appointed counsel for petty offenses for which imprisonment will not be imposed or when the defendant is financially able to retain counsel; it further understands that subparagraph (2)(f) does not forbid requiring an indigent defendant to make a showing that the witness is necessary in order for his attendance to be compelled by the court. The United States understands that the prohibition on double jeopardy contained in paragraph (4) is applicable only when the judgment of acquittal has been rendered by a court of the same governmental unit, whether the Federal Government or a constituent unit, which is seeking a new trial for the same cause."

Article 9 prohibits *ex post facto* criminal laws, and requires as well that the benefit of any statutory reductions in the penalty for crimes be applied retroactively. The latter provision, which goes beyond existing United States law, necessitates a reservation as follows:

"The United States does not adhere to the third sentence of Article 9."

Article 10 provides for the right to compensation in the event of a sentence imposed through "a miscarriage of justice." United States law provides only a limited right to recovery, available to innocent persons who have been unjustly convicted and imprisoned, and not to those whose improper conviction was due to procedural errors alone. The Senate may wish to record its understanding that the United States Code, Title 28, §§ 1495 and 2513, meets the requirements of Article 10.

Article 11 protects the right to privacy. Article 12 provides for freedom of conscience and religion, subject to legal limitations "necessary to protect public safety, health, or morals, or the rights or freedoms of others."

Article 13 protects freedom of thought and expression, including the right to seek, receive, and impart information and ideas of all kinds, regardless of frontiers. Paragraph (2) of Article 13 states that these rights "shall not be subject to prior censorship" but shall be subject to subsequent imposition of liability in order to ensure respect for the rights or reputations of others, or the protection of national security, public order, health or morals.

Paragraph (3) of Article 13 provides that the right of expression may not be restricted by indirect methods, such as the abuse of government or private controls over information media. Under paragraph (4), public entertainment may be subject by law to prior censorship "for the moral protection of childhood and adolescence."

Paragraph (5) of Article 13 stipulates that "any propaganda for war and any advocacy of national, racial, or religious hatred that constitute incitements to lawless violence or to any other similar illegal action against any person or group of persons on any grounds including those of race, color, religion, language, or national origin shall be considered as offenses punishable by law."

Both paragraph (2) and paragraph (5) of Article 13 raise questions under the First Amendment and of consistency with United States law. The following reservation is recommended:

"The United States reserves the right to permit prior restraints in strictly defined circumstances where the right to judicial review is immediately available; the United States does not adhere to paragraph (5) of Article 13."

Article 14, on the right of reply, provides:

1. Anyone injured by inaccurate or offensive statements or ideas disseminated to the public in general by a legally regulated medium of communication has the right to reply or make a correction using the same communications outlet, under such conditions as the law may establish.
2. The correction or reply shall not in any case remit other legal liabilities that may have been incurred.
3. For the effective protection of honor and reputation, every publisher, and every newspaper, motion picture, radio, and television company, shall have a person responsible, who is not protected by immunities or special privileges.

Under United States law the "fairness doctrine," applicable to radio and television, is narrower than the right provided by paragraph (1) of Article 14. Further, paragraph (3) does not reflect the sovereign immunity granted government publishers under United States law. The following reservation and understanding are recommended:

"The United States does not adhere to paragraph (1) of Article 14, and understands that paragraph (3) of that Article applies only to non-governmental entities."

Article 15 guarantees the right of assembly and Article 16 the right of freedom of association. Both rights may be limited by established law "in the interest of national security, public safety or public order, or to protect public health or morals or the rights and freedoms of others."

Article 17, on the rights of the family, requires that the family unit be protected by society and the State. No marriage is to be entered into without the free and full consent of the intending spouses. Paragraphs (4) and (5) forbid discrimination against illegitimate children and obligate States to take steps to eliminate discrimination between spouses during marriage and in the event of its dissolution. Both paragraphs state goals towards which United States law is moving, but neither goal has been fully achieved. The following statement is recommended:

"The United States considers the provisions of paragraphs (4) and (5) of Article 17 as goals to be achieved progressively rather than through immediate implementation."

Articles 18 and 19 protect the right to a name and the rights of the child in general terms. Article 20 protects the right to nationality. Article 21 stipulates that everyone has the right to the use and enjoyment of his property but that the law may subordinate such use and enjoyment to the interest of society. However, paragraph (2) of Article 21 provides that "no one shall be deprived of his property except upon payment of just compensation for reasons of public utility or social interest and in the cases and according to the forms established by law."

Article 22 of the Convention provides for freedom of movement and residence. It stipulates that every person lawfully in the territory of a State Party has the right to move about within that territory, and to reside in it or to depart it, with limitation only pursuant to law and for the purposes of preventing crime or protecting national security, public safety, order, morals, health, or the rights or freedoms of others. An alien lawfully in the territory of a State Party may be expelled only pursuant to a decision reached in accordance with law. The collective expulsion of aliens is prohibited. Paragraph (7) grants a right of territorial asylum in accordance with law and international conventions.

Paragraph (8) of Article 22 states that in no case may an alien be deported or returned to a country in which his life or freedom would be endangered because of his race, nationality, religion, social status or political opinions. United States law and the Protocol Relating to the Status of Refugees, to which the United States is party, permit immigration officers, in their discretion, to deport persons even to countries in which their lives or freedom are so threatened if such persons have committed a serious crime or are considered a danger to the security of this country. The following statement is recommended:

"The United States considers that its adherence to the Protocol Relating to the Status of Refugees constitutes compliance with the obligation set forth in paragraph (8) of Article 22."

Article 23 protects the right to participate in government, including voting in "genuine periodic elections" by universal and equal suffrage, and access to the public service of the

country. Article 24 is a general clause providing for the right
to equal protection of the law. Article 25 secures the right to
judicial protection.

Article 26 is the only provision in the American Convention devoted to economic, social, and cultural rights. It requires States Parties to adopt measures, particularly those of
an economic and technical nature, "with a view to achieving
progressively, by legislation or other appropriate means, the
full realization of the rights implicit in the economic, social,
educational, scientific, and cultural standards set forth in the
Charter of the Organization of American States as amended
by the Protocol of Buenos Aires."

Article 27 permits a suspension of the guarantees provided in the Convention during time of war, public danger
or other emergencies that threaten the independence or security of a State Party. The derogation must not involve discrimination on the ground of race, color, sex, language,
religion, or social origin. In addition, no suspension is permitted with respect to Articles 3 through 6, 9, 12, 17 through
20, and 23, or to the judicial guarantees essential for the
protection of such rights.

Article 28 is the federal State clause, which takes account
of and is in the interest of federal systems such as the United
States. It provides that the national government is to implement those provisions of the Convention over whose subject
matter it exercises legislative and judicial jurisdiction. Where
the several states have jurisdiction, the national government
is to take "suitable measures" in accordance with its constitution and laws, to the end that the state authorities "may
adopt appropriate provisions" for the fulfillment of the
terms of the Convention.

The second half of the American Convention, including
Articles 33 through 82, establishes machinery for monitoring compliance. The Inter-American Commission
on Human Rights is empowered to receive complaints from
individuals or groups or, upon appropriate declaration,
from States regarding violations of the rights protected by
the Convention.

Petitions or communications are not admissible unless domestic law remedies have been exhausted. The Commis-

sion's powers are limited to requesting information from the
State whose compliance with the Convention is in question,
requesting assistance for the carrying out of any necessary
investigation, and making recommendations and releasing
to the public reports on unresolved cases.

Should the Senate give its advice and consent to ratification of the Convention, it is contemplated that the United
States will make a declaration pursuant to Article 45, which
permits, but does not require, a declaration recognizing the
competence of the Commission "to receive and examine
communications in which a State Party alleges that another
State Party has committed a violation of a human right set
forth in this Convention." As with the United Nations Covenant on Civil and Political Rights, it is in the interest of the
United States to participate in and influence the State-to-
State complaint procedure.

The enforcement machinery of the Convention includes
as well an Inter-American Court of Human Rights which
gains jurisdiction over cases by the voluntary declaration of
States. Cases may also be submitted by special agreement
between the parties to a dispute. Acceptance by the United
States of the Court's jurisdiction, whether by means of a voluntary declaration or by a special agreement, would of
course require separate Senate advice and consent. The
Court, which votes by majority, has power to require that the
injured party be ensured the enjoyment of the freedom violated, and, if appropriate, it may require the payment of
compensation. It may issue temporary or permanent injunc-
tions in all cases concerning the interpretation and application of the provisions of the Convention. States Parties to the
Convention undertake to obey judgments of the Court in
cases to which they are parties.

The American Convention on Human Rights is a significant advance in the development of the international law of
human rights and in the development of human rights law
among the American States. United States ratification of the
Convention is likely to spur interest in this important document among other American States. United States adherence is in the national interest and in that of the world
community. It is our hope that the Senate, after full consid-

eration, will give prompt approval to the Convention, and
that the United States will become a party to it.

Respectfully submitted.

WARREN CHRISTOPHER.

International Convention on the Elimination of All Forms of Racial Discrimination

*   *   *

The States Parties to this Convention,

Considering that the Charter of the United Nations is based on the principles of the dignity and equality inherent in all human beings, and that all Member States have pledged themselves to take joint and separate action, in co-operation with the Organization, for the achievement of one of the purposes of the United Nations which is to promote and encourage universal respect for and observance of human rights and fundamental freedoms for all, without distinction as to race, sex, language or religion,

Considering that the Universal Declaration of Human Rights proclaims that all human beings are born free and equal in dignity and rights and that everyone is entitled to all the rights and freedoms set out therein, without distinction of any kind, in particular as to race, colour or national origin,

Considering that all human beings are equal before the law and are entitled to equal protection of the law against any discrimination and against any incitement to discrimination,

Considering that the United Nations has condemned colonialism and all practices of segregation and discrimination associated therewith, in whatever form and wherever they exist, and that the Declaration on the Granting of Independence to Colonial Countries and Peoples of 14 December 1960 (General Assembly resolution 1514 (XV)) has affirmed and solemnly proclaimed the necessity of bringing them to a speedy and unconditional end,

Considering that the United Nations Declaration on the Elimination of All Forms of Racial Discrimination of 20 November 1963 (General Assembly resolution 1904 (XVIII)) solemnly affirms the necessity of speedily eliminating racial discrimination throughout the world in all its forms and manifestations and of securing understanding of and respect for the dignity of the human person,

Convinced that any doctrine of superiority based on racial differentiation is scientifically false, morally condemnable, socially unjust and dangerous, and that there is no justification for racial discrimination, in theory or in practice, anywhere,

Reaffirming that discrimination between human beings on the grounds of race, colour or ethnic origin is an obstacle to friendly and peaceful relations among nations and is capable of disturbing peace and security among peoples and the harmony of persons living side by side even within one and the same State,

Convinced that the existence of racial barriers is repugnant to the ideals of any human society,

Alarmed by manifestations of racial discrimination still in evidence in some areas of the world and by governmental policies based on racial superiority or hatred, such as policies of *apartheid*, segregation or separation,

Resolved to adopt all necessary measures for speedily eliminating racial discrimination in all its forms and manifestations, and to prevent and combat racist doctrines and practices in order to promote understanding between races and to build an international community free from all forms of racial segregation and racial discrimination,

Bearing in mind the Convention concerning Discrimination in respect of Employment and Occupation adopted by the International Labour Organisation in 1958, and the Convention against Discrimination in Education adopted by the United Nations Educational, Scientific and Cultural Organisation in 1960,

Desiring to implement the principles embodied in the United Nations Declaration on the Elimination of All Forms of Racial Discrimination and to secure the earliest adoption of practical measures to that end,

Have agreed as follows:

PART I
Article 1

1. In this Convention, the term "racial discrimination" shall mean any distinction, exclusion, restriction or preference based on race, colour, descent, or national or ethnic origin which has the purpose or effect of nullifying or impairing the recognition, enjoyment or exercise, on an equal footing, of human rights and fundamental freedoms in the political, economic, social, cultural or any other field of public life.

2. This Convention shall not apply to distinctions, exclusions, restrictions or preferences made by a State Party to this Convention between citizens and noncitizens.

3. Nothing in this Convention may be interpreted as affecting in any way the legal provisions of States Parties concerning nationality, citizenship or naturalization, provided that such provisions do not discriminate against any particular nationality.

4. Special measures taken for the sole purpose of securing adequate advancement of certain racial or ethnic groups or individuals requiring such protection as may be necessary in order to ensure such groups or individuals equal enjoyment or exercise of human rights and fundamental freedoms shall not be deemed racial discrimination, provided, however, that such measures do not, as a consequence, lead to the maintenance of separate rights for different racial groups and that they shall not be continued after the objectives for which they were taken have been achieved.

Article 2

1. States Parties condemn racial discrimination and undertake to pursue by all appropriate means and without delay a policy of eliminating racial discrimination in all its forms and promoting understanding among all races, and, to this end:

(*a*) Each State Party undertakes to engage in no act or practice of racial discrimination against persons, groups of persons or institutions and to ensure that all public authorities and public institutions, national and local, shall act in conformity with this obligation;

(*b*) Each State Party undertakes not to sponsor, defend or support racial discrimination by any persons or organizations;

(*c*) Each State Party shall take effective measures to review governmental, national and local policies, and to amend, rescind or nullify any laws and regulations which have the effect of creating or perpetuating racial discrimination wherever it exists;

(*d*) Each State Party shall prohibit and bring to an end, by all appropriate means, including legislation as required by circumstances, racial discrimination by any persons, group or organization;

(*e*) Each State Party undertakes to encourage, where appropriate, integrationist multi-racial organizations and movements and other means of eliminating barriers between races, and to discourage anything which tends to strengthen racial division.

2. States Parties shall when the circumstances so warrant, take, in the social, economic, cultural and other fields, special and concrete measures to ensure the adequate development and protection of certain racial groups or individuals belonging to them, for the purpose of guaranteeing them the full and equal enjoyment of human rights and fundamental freedoms. These measures shall in no case entail as a consequence the maintenance of unequal or separate rights for different racial groups after the objectives for which they were taken have been achieved.

Article 3

State Parties particularly condemn racial segregation and *apartheid* and undertake to prevent, prohibit and eradicate all practices of this nature in territories under their jurisdiction.

Article 4

State Parties condemn all propaganda and all organizations which are based on ideas or theories of superiority of one race or group of persons of one colour or ethnic origin,

or which attempt to justify or promote racial hatred and
discrimination in any form, and undertake to adopt immediate and positive measures designed to eradicate all incitement to, or acts of, such discrimination and, to this end, with
due regard to the principles embodied in the Universal Declaration of Human Rights and the rights expressly set forth
in article 5 of this Convention, *inter alia*:

(a) Shall declare an offence punishable by law all dissemination of ideas based on racial superiority or hatred,
incitement to discrimination, as well as all acts of violence
or incitement to such acts against any race or group of
persons of another colour or ethnic origin, and also the
provision of any assistance to racist activities, including
the financing thereof;

(b) Shall declare illegal and prohibit organizations, and
also organized and all other propaganda activities, which
promote and incite racial discrimination, and shall recognize participation in such organizations or activities as an
offence punishable by law;

(c) Shall not permit public authorities or public institutions, national or local, to promote or incite racial discrimination.

Article 5

In compliance with the fundamental obligations laid down
in article 2 of this Convention, States Parties undertake to
prohibit and to eliminate racial discrimination in all its forms
and to guarantee the right of everyone, without distinction
as to race, colour, or national or ethnic origin, to equality
before the law, notably in the enjoyment of the following
rights:

(a) The right to equal treatment before the tribunals
and all other organs administering justice;

(b) The right to security of person and protection by
the State against violence or bodily harm, whether inflicted by government officials or by any individual group
or institution;

(c) Political rights, in particular the rights to participate
in elections—to vote and to stand for election—on the ba-

sis of universal and equal suffrage, to take part in the Government as well as in the conduct of public affairs at any level and to have equal access to public service;

(*d*) Other civil rights, in particular:

(i) The right to freedom of movement and residence within the border of the State;

(ii) The right to leave any country, including one's own, and to return to one's country;

(iii) The right to nationality;

(iv) The right to marriage and choice of spouse;

(v) The right to own property alone as well as in association with others;

(vi) The right to inherit;

(vii) The right to freedom of thought, conscience and religion;

(viii) The right to freedom of opinion and expression;

(ix) The right to freedom of peaceful assembly and association;

(*e*) Economic, social and cultural rights, in particular:

(i) The right to work, to free choice of employment, to just and favourable conditions of work, to protection against unemployment, to equal pay for equal work, to just and favourable remuneration;

(ii) The right to form and join trade unions;

(iii) The right to housing;

(iv) The right to public health, medical care, social security and social services;

(v) The right to education and training;

(vi) The right to equal participation in cultural activities;

(*f*) The right of access to any place or service intended for use by the general public, such as transport, hotels, restaurants, cafés, theatres and parks.

Article 6

States Parties shall assure to everyone within their jurisdiction effective protection and remedies, through the competent national tribunals and other State institutions, against any acts of racial discrimination which violate his human rights and fundamental freedoms contrary to this Convention, as well as the right to seek from such tribunals just and adequate reparation or satisfaction for any damage suffered as a result of such discrimination.

Article 7

States Parties undertake to adopt immediate and effective measures, particularly in the fields of teaching, education, culture and information, with a view to combating prejudices which lead to racial discrimination and to promoting understanding, tolerance and friendship among nations and racial or ethnical groups, as well as to propagating the purposes and principles of the Charter of the United Nations, the Universal Declaration of Human Rights, the United Nations Declaration on the Elimination of All Forms of Racial Discrimination, and this Convention.

PART II
Article 8

1. There shall be established a Committee on the Elimination of Racial Discrimination (hereinafter referred to as the Committee) consisting of eighteen experts of high moral standing and acknowledged impartiality elected by States Parties from among their nationals, who shall serve in their personal capacity, consideration being given to equitable geographical distribution and to the representation of the different forms of civilization as well as of the principal legal systems.

2. The members of the Committee shall be elected by secret ballot from a list of persons nominated by the States Parties. Each State Party may nominate one person from among its own nationals.

3. The initial election shall be held six months after the date of the entry into force of this Convention. At least three months before the date of each election the Secretary-General of the United Nations shall address a letter to the States Parties inviting them to submit their nominations within two months. The Secretary-General shall prepare a list in alpha-

betical order of all persons thus nominated, indicating the States Parties which have nominated them, and shall submit it to the States Parties.

4. Elections of the members of the Committee shall be held at a meeting of States Parties convened by the Secretary-General at United Nations Headquarters. At that meeting, for which two thirds of the States Parties shall constitute a quorum, the persons elected to the Committee shall be those nominees who obtain the largest number of votes and an absolute majority of the votes of the representatives of States Parties present and voting.

5. (*a*) The members of the Committee shall be elected for a term of four years. However, the terms of nine of the members elected at the first election shall expire at the end of two years; immediately after the first election the names of these nine members shall be chosen by lot by the Chairman of the Committee.

(*b*) For the filling of casual vacancies, the State Party whose expert has ceased to function as a member of the Committee shall appoint another expert from among its nationals, subject to the approval of the Committee.

6. States Parties shall be responsible for the expenses of the members of the Committee while they are in performance of Committee duties.

Article 9

1. States Parties undertake to submit to the Secretary-General of the United Nations, for consideration by the Committee, a report on the legislative, judicial, administrative or other measures which they have adopted and which give effect to the provisions of this Convention: (*a*) within one year after the entry into force of the Convention for the State concerned; and (*b*) thereafter every two years and whenever the Committee so requests. The Committee may request further information from the States Parties.

2. The Committee shall report annually, through the Secretary-General, to the General Assembly of the United Nations on its activities and may make suggestions and general recommendations based on the examination of the reports

and information received from the States Parties. Such suggestions and general recommendations shall be reported to the General Assembly together with comments, if any, from States Parties.

Article 10

1. The Committee shall adopt its own rules of procedure.
2. The Committee shall elect its officers for a term of two years.
3. The secretariat of the Committee shall be provided by the Secretary-General of the United Nations.
4. The meetings of the Committee shall normally be held at United Nations Headquarters.

Article 11

1. If a State Party considers that another State Party is not giving effect to the provisions of this Convention, it may bring the matter to the attention of the Committee. The Committee shall then transmit the communication to the State Party concerned. Within three months, the receiving State shall submit to the Committee written explanations or statements clarifying the matter and the remedy, if any, that may have been taken by that State.
2. If the matter is not adjusted to the satisfaction of both parties, either by bilateral negotiations or by any other procedure open to them, within six months after the receipt by the receiving State of the initial communication, either State shall have the right to refer the matter again to the Committee by notifying the Committee and also the other State.
3. The Committee shall deal with a matter referred to it in accordance with paragraph 2 of this article after it has ascertained that all available domestic remedies have been invoked and exhausted in the case, in conformity with the generally recognized principles of international law. This shall not be the rule where the application of the remedies is unreasonably prolonged.
4. In any matter referred to it, the Committee may call upon the States Parties concerned to supply any other relevant information.
5. When any matter arising out of this article is being

considered by the Committee, the States Parties concerned shall be entitled to send a representative to take part in the proceedings of the Committee, without voting rights, while the matter is under consideration.

Article 12

1. (*a*) After the Committee has obtained and collated all the information it deems necessary, the Chairman shall appoint an *ad hoc* Conciliation Commission (herein-after referred to as the Commission) comprising five persons who may or may not be members of the Committee. The members of the Commission shall be appointed with the unanimous consent of the parties to the dispute, and its good offices shall be made available to the States concerned with a view to an amicable solution of the matter on the basis of respect for this Convention.

(*b*) If the States parties to the dispute fail to reach agreement within three months on all or part of the composition of the Commission, the members of the Commission not agreed upon by the States parties to the dispute shall be elected by secret ballot by a two-thirds majority vote on the Committee from among its own members.

2. The members of the Commission shall serve in their personal capacity. They shall not be nationals of the States parties to the dispute or of a State not Party to this Convention.

3. The Commission shall elect its own Chairman and adopt its own rules of procedure.

4. The meetings of the Commission shall normally be held at United Nations Headquarters or at any other convenient place as determined by the Commission.

5. The secretariat provided in accordance with article 10, paragraph 3, of this Convention shall also service the Commission whenever a dispute among States Parties brings the Commission into being.

6. The States parties to the dispute shall share equally all the expenses of the members of the Commission in accordance with estimates to be provided by the Secretary-General of the United Nations.

7. The Secretary-General shall be empowered to pay the

expenses of the members to the Commission, if necessary, before reimbursement by the States parties to the dispute in accordance with paragraph 6 of this article.

8. The information obtained and collated by the Committee shall be made available to the Commission, and the Commission may call upon the States concerned to supply any other relevant information.

Article 13

1. When the Commission has fully considered the matter, it shall prepare and submit to the Chairman of the Committee a report embodying its findings on all questions of fact relevant to the issue between the parties and containing such recommendations as it may think proper for the amicable solution of the dispute.

2. The Chairman of the Committee shall communicate the report of the Commission to each of the States parties to the dispute. These States shall, within three months, inform the Chairman of the Committee whether or not they accept the recommendations contained in the report of the Commission.

3. After the period provided for in paragraph 2 of this article, the Chairman of the Committee shall communicate the report of the Commission and the declarations of the States Parties concerned to the other States Parties to this Convention.

Article 14

1. A State Party may at any time declare that it recognizes the competence of the Committee to receive and consider communications from individuals or groups of individuals within its jurisdiction claiming to be victims of a violation by that State Party of any of the rights set forth in this Convention. No communication shall be received by the Committee if it concerns a State Party which has not made such a declaration.

2. Any State Party which makes a declaration as provided for in paragraph 1 of this article may establish or indicate a body within its national legal order which shall be competent

to receive and consider petitions from individuals and groups of individuals within its jurisdiction who claim to be victims of a violation of any of the rights set forth in this Convention and who have exhausted other available local remedies.

3. A declaration made in accordance with paragraph 1 of this article and the name of any body established or indicated in accordance with paragraph 2 of this article shall be deposited by the State Party concerned with the Secretary-General of the United Nations, who shall transmit copies thereof to the other States Parties. A declaration may be withdrawn at any time by notification to the Secretary-General, but such a withdrawal shall not affect communications pending before the Committee.

4. A register of petitions shall be kept by the body established or indicated in accordance with paragraph 2 of this article, and certified copies of the register shall be filled annually through appropriate channels with the Secretary-General on the understanding that the contents shall not be publicly disclosed.

5. In the event of failure to obtain satisfaction from the body established or indicated in accordance with paragraph 2 of this article, the petitioner shall have the right to communicate the matter to the Committee within six months.

6. (*a*) The Committee shall confidentially bring any communication referred to it to the attention of the State Party alleged to be violating any provision of this Convention, but the identity of the individual or groups of individuals concerned shall not be revealed without his or their express consent. The Committee shall not receive anonymous communications.

(*b*) Within three months, the receiving State shall submit to the Committee written explanations or statements clarifying the matter and the remedy, if any, that may have been taken by that State.

7. (*a*) The Committee shall consider communications in the light of all information made available to it by the State Party concerned and by the petitioner. The Committee shall not consider any communication from a petitioner unless it

has ascertained that the petitioner has exhausted all available domestic remedies. However, this shall not be the rule where the application of the remedies is unreasonably prolonged.

(*b*) The Committee shall forward its suggestions and recommendations, if any, to the State Party concerned and to the petitioner.

8. The Committee shall include in its annual report a summary of such communications and, where appropriate, a summary of the explanations and statements of the States Parties concerned and of its own suggestions and recommendations.

9. The Committee shall be competent to exercise the functions provided for in this article only when at least ten States Parties to this Convention are bound by declarations in accordance with paragraph 1 of this article.

Article 15

1. Pending the achievement of the objectives of the Declaration on the Granting of Independence to Colonial Countries and Peoples, contained in General Assembly resolution 1514(XV) of 14 December 1960, the provisions of this Convention shall in no way limit the right of petition granted to these peoples by other international instruments or by the United Nations and its specialized agencies.

2. (*a*) The Committee established under article 8, paragraph 1, of this Convention shall receive copies of the petitions from, and submit expressions of opinion and recommendations on these petitions to, the bodies of the United Nations which deal with matters directly related to the principles and objectives of this Convention in their consideration of petitions from the inhabitants of Trust and Non-Self-Governing Territories and all other territories to which General Assembly resolution 1514 (XV) applies, relating to matters covered by this Convention which are before these bodies.

(*b*) The Committee shall receive from the competent bodies of the United Nations copies of the reports concerning the legislative, judicial, administrative or other measures directly related to the principles and objectives of this Convention applied by the administering Powers within the Territories mentioned in subparagraph (*a*) of this paragraph, and shall express opinions and make recommendations to these bodies.

3. The Committee shall include in its report to the General Assembly a summary of the petitions and reports it has received from United Nations bodies, and the expressions of opinion and recommendations of the Committee relating to the said petitions and reports.

4. The Committee shall request from the Secretary-General of the United Nations all information relevant to the objectives of this Convention and available to him regarding the Territories mentioned in paragraph 2(*a*) of this article.

Article 16

The provisions of this Convention concerning the settlement of disputes or complaints shall be applied without prejudice to other procedures for settling disputes or complaints in the field of discrimination laid down in the constituent instruments of, or in conventions adopted by, the United Nations and its specialized agencies, and shall not prevent the States Parties from having recourse to other procedures for settling a dispute in accordance with general or special international agreements in force between them.

PART III
Article 17

1. This Convention is open for signature by any State Member of the United Nations or member of any of its specialized agencies, by any State Party to the Statute of the International Court of Justice, and by any other State which has been invited by the General Assembly of the United Nations to become a Party to this Convention.

2. This Convention is subject to ratification. Instruments of ratification shall be deposited with the Secretary-General of the United Nations.

Article 18

1. This Convention shall be open to accession by any State referred to in article 17, paragraph 1, of the Convention.

2. Accession shall be effected by the deposit of an instrument of accession with the Secretary-General of the United Nations.

Article 19

1. This Convention shall enter into force on the thirtieth day after the date of the deposit with the Secretary-General of the United Nations of the twenty-seventh instrument of ratification or instrument of accession.

2. For each State ratifying this Convention or acceding to it after the deposit of the twenty-seventh instrument of ratification or instrument of accession, the Convention shall enter into force on the thirtieth day after the date of the deposit of its own instrument of ratification or instrument of accession.

Article 20

1. The Secretary-General of the United Nations shall receive and circulate to all States which are or may become Parties to this Convention reservations made by States at the time of ratification or accession. Any State which objects to the reservation shall, within a period of ninety days from the date of the said communication, notify the Secretary-General that it does not accept it.

2. A reservation incompatible with the object and purpose of this Convention shall not be permitted, nor shall a reservation the effect of which would inhibit the operation of any of the bodies established by this Convention be allowed. A reservation shall be considered incompatible or inhibitive if at least two thirds of the States Parties to this Convention object to it.

3. Reservations may be withdrawn at any time by notification to this effect addressed to the Secretary-General. Such notification shall take effect on the date on which it is received.

Article 21

A State Party may denounce this Convention by written notification to the Secretary-General of the United Nations. Denunciation shall take effect one year after the date of receipt of the notification by the Secretary-General.

Article 22

Any dispute between two or more States Parties with respect to the interpretation or application of this Convention, which is not settled by negotiation or by the procedures expressly provided for in this Convention, shall, at the request of any of the parties to the dispute, be referred to the International Court of Justice for decision, unless the disputants agree to another mode of settlement.

Article 23

1. A request for the revision of this Convention may be made at any time by any State Party by means of a notification in writing addressed to the Secretary-General of the United Nations.
2. The General Assembly of the United Nations shall decide upon the steps, if any, to be taken in respect of such a request.

Article 24

The Secretary-General of the United Nations shall inform all States referred to in article 17, paragraph 1, of this Convention of the following particulars:

(*a*) Signatures, ratifications and accessions under articles 17 and 18;

(*b*) The date of entry into force of this Convention under article 19;

(*c*) Communications and declarations received under articles 14, 20 and 23;

(*d*) Denunciations under article 21.

Article 25

1. This Convention, of which the Chinese, English, French, Russian and Spanish texts are equally authentic, shall be deposited in the archives of the United Nations.

2. The Secretary-General of the United Nations shall transmit certified copies of this Convention to all States belonging to any of the categories mentioned in article 17, paragraph 1, of the Convention.

International Covenant on Economic, Social, and Cultural Rights

*   *   *

Preamble

The States Parties to the present Covenant,

Considering that, in accordance with the principles proclaimed in the Charter of the United Nations, recognition of the inherent dignity and of the equal and inalienable rights of all members of the human family is the foundation of freedom, justice and peace in the world,

Recognizing that these rights derive from the inherent dignity of the human person,

Recognizing that, in accordance with the Universal Declaration of Human Rights, the ideal of free human beings enjoying freedom from fear and want can only be achieved if conditions are created whereby everyone may enjoy his economic, social and cultural rights, as well as his civil and political rights,

Considering the obligation of States under the Charter of the United Nations to promote universal respect for, and observance of, human rights and freedoms.

Realizing that the individual, having duties to other individuals and to the community to which he belongs, is under a responsibility to strive for the promotion and observance of the rights recognized in the present Covenant,

Agree upon the following articles:

PART I
Article 1

1. All peoples have the right of self-determination. By virtue of the right they freely determine their political status

and freely pursue their economic, social and cultural development.

2. All peoples may, for their own ends, freely dispose of their natural wealth and resources without prejudice to any obligations arising out of international economic co-operation, based upon the principle of mutual benefit, and international law. In no case may a people be deprived of its own means of subsistence.

3. The States Parties to the present Covenant, including those having responsibility for the administration of Non-Self-Governing and Trust Territories, shall promote the realization of the right of self-determination, and shall respect that right, in conformity with the provisions of the United Nations Charter.

PART II
Article 2

1. Each State Party to the present Covenant undertakes to take steps, individually and through international assistance and cooperation especially economic and technical, to the maximum of its available resources, with a view to achieving progressively the full realization of the rights recognized in the present Covenant by all appropriate means, including particularly the adoption of legislative measures.

2. The States Parties to the present Covenant undertake to guarantee that the rights enunciated in the present Covenant will be exercised without discrimination of any kind as to race, colour, sex, language, religion, political or other opinion, national or social origin, property, birth or other status.

3. Developing countries, with due regard to human rights and their national economy, may determine to what extent they would guarantee the economic rights recognized in the present Covenant to non-nationals.

Article 3

The States Parties to the present Covenant undertake to ensure the equal right of men and women to the enjoyment of all economic, social and cultural rights set forth in this Covenant.

Article 4

The States Parties to the present Covenant recognize that in the enjoyment of those rights provided by the State in conformity with the present Covenant, the State may subject such rights only to such limitations as are determined by law only in so far as this may be compatible with the nature of these rights and solely for the purpose of promoting the general welfare in a democratic society.

Article 5

1. Nothing in the present Covenant may be interpreted as implying for any State, group or person, any right to engage in any activity or to perform any act aimed at the destruction of any of the rights or freedoms recognized herein, or at their limitation to a greater extent than is provided for in the present Covenant.

2. No restriction upon or derogation from any of the fundamental human rights recognized or existing in any country in virtue of law, conventions, regulations or custom shall be admitted on the pretext that the present Covenant does not recognize such rights or that it recognizes them to a lesser extent.

PART III
Article 6

1. The States Parties to the present Covenant recognize the right to work, which includes the right of everyone to the opportunity to gain his living by work which he freely chooses or accepts, and will take appropriate steps to safeguard this right.

2. The steps to be taken by a State Party to the present Covenant to achieve the full realization of this right shall include technical and vocational guidance and training programmes, policies and techniques to achieve steady economic, social and cultural development and full and productive employment under conditions safeguarding fundamental political and economic freedoms to the individual.

Article 7

The States Parties to the present Covenant recognize the right of everyone to the enjoyment of just and favourable conditions of work, which ensure, in particular:

(a) Remuneration which provides all workers as a minimum with:

   (i) Fair wages and equal remuneration for work of equal value without distinction of any kind, in particular women being guaranteed conditions of work not inferior to those enjoyed by men, with equal pay for equal work; and

   (ii) A decent living for themselves and their families in accordance with the provisions of the present Covenant;

(b) Safe and healthy working conditions;

(c) Equal opportunity for everyone to be promoted in his employment to an appropriate higher level, subject to no considerations other than those of seniority and competence;

(d) Rest, leisure and reasonable limitation of working hours and periodic holidays with pay, as well as remuneration for public holidays.

Article 8

1. The States Parties to the present Covenant undertake to ensure:

(a) The right of everyone to form trade unions and join the trade union of his choice subject only to the rules of the organization concerned, for the promotion and protection of his economic and social interests. No restrictions may be placed on the exercise of this right other than those prescribed by law and which are necessary in a democratic society in the interests of national security or public order or for the protection of the rights and freedom of others;

(b) The right of trade unions to establish national federations or confederations and the right of the latter to form or join international trade-union organizations;

(*c*) The right of trade unions to function freely subject to no limitations other than those prescribed by law and which are necessary in a democratic society in the interests of national security or public order or for the protection of the rights and freedoms of others;

(*d*) The right to strike, provided that it is exercised in conformity with the laws of the particular country.

2. This article shall not prevent the imposition of lawful restrictions on the exercise of these rights by members of the armed forces, or of the police, or of the administration of the State.

3. Nothing in this article shall authorize States Parties to the International Labour Convention of 1948 on Freedom of Association and Protection of the Rights to Organize to take legislative measures which would prejudice, or apply the law in such a manner as would prejudice, the guarantees provided for in that Convention.

Article 9

The States Parties to the present Covenant recognize the right of everyone to social security including social insurance.

Article 10

The States Parties to the present Covenant recognize that:

1. The widest possible protection and assistance should be accorded to the family, which is the natural and fundamental group unit of society, particulary for its establishment and while it is responsible for the care and education of dependent children. Marriage must be entered into with the free consent of the intending spouses;

2. Special protection should be accorded to mothers during a reasonable period before and after childbirth. During such period working mothers should be accorded paid leave or leave with adequate social security benefits;

3. Special measures of protection and assistance should be taken on behalf of all children and young persons without any discrimination for reasons of parentage or other conditions. Children and young persons should be protected from economic and social exploitation. Their employment in work

harmful to their morals or health or dangerous to life or likely to hamper their normal development should be punishable by law. States should also set age limits below which the paid employment of child labour should be prohibited and punishable by law.

Article 11

1. The States Parties to the present Covenant recognize the right of everyone to an adequate standard of living for himself and his family, including adequate food, clothing and housing, and to the continuous improvement of living conditions. The States Parties will take appropriate steps to ensure the realization of this right, recognizing to this effect the essential importance of international co-operation based on free consent.

2. The States Parties to the present Covenant, recognizing the fundamental right of everyone to be free from hunger, shall take, individually and through international co-operation, the measures, including specific programmes, which are needed:

(*a*) To improve methods of production, conservation and distribution of food by making full use of technical and scientific knowledge, by disseminating knowledge of the principles of nutrition and by developing or reforming agrarian systems in such a way as to achieve the most efficient development and utilization of natural resources; and

(*b*) Take into account the problems of both food-importing and food-exporting countries, to ensure an equitable distribution of world food supplies in relation to need.

Article 12

1. The States Parties to the present Covenant recognize the right of everyone to the enjoyment of the highest attainable standard of physical and mental health.

2. The steps to be taken by the States Parties to the present Covenant to achieve the full realization of this right shall include those necessary for:

(*a*) The provision for the reduction of the still-birth-rate and of infant mortality and for the healthy development of the child;

(*b*) The improvement of all aspects of environmental and industrial hygiene;

(*c*) The prevention, treatment and control of epidemic, endemic, occupational and other diseases;

(*d*) The creation of conditions which would assure to all medical service and medical attention in the event of sickness.

Article 13

1. The States Parties to the present Covenant recognize the right of everyone to education. They agree that education shall be directed to the full development of the human personality and the sense of its dignity, and shall strengthen the respect for human rights and fundamental freedoms. They further agree that education shall enable all persons to participate effectively in a free society, promote understanding, tolerance and friendship among all nations and all racial, ethnic or religious groups, and further the activities of the United Nations for the maintenance of peace.

2. The States Parties to the present Covenant recognize that, with a view to achieving the full realization of this right:

(*a*) Primary education shall be compulsory and available free to all;

(*b*) Secondary education in its different forms, including technical and vocational secondary education, shall be made generally available and accessible to all by every appropriate means, and in particular by the progressive introduction of free education;

(*c*) Higher education shall be made equally accessible to all, on the basis of capacity, by every appropriate means, and in particular by the progressive introduction of free education;

(*d*) Fundamental education shall be encouraged or intensified as far as possible for those persons who have not received or completed the whole period of their primary education;

(*e*) The development of a system of schools at all levels shall be actively pursued, an adequate fellowship system shall be established, and the material conditions of teaching staff shall be continuously improved.

3. The States Parties to the present Covenant undertake to have respect for the liberty of parents and, when applicable, legal guardians, to choose for their children schools other than those established by the public authorities which conform to such minimum educational standards as may be laid down or approved by the State and to ensure the religious and moral education of their children in conformity with their own convictions.

4. No part of this article shall be construed so as to interfere with the liberty of individuals and bodies to establish and direct educational institutions, subject always to the observance of the principles set forth in paragraph 1 and to the requirement that the education given in such institutions shall conform to such minimum standards as may be laid down by the State.

Article 14

Each State Party to the present Covenant which, at the time of becoming a Party, has not been able to secure in its metropolitan territory or other territories under its jurisdiction compulsory primary education, free of charge, undertakes, within two years, to work out and adopt a detailed plan of action for the progressive implementation, within a reasonable number of years, to be fixed in the plan, of the principle of compulsory education free of charge for all.

Article 15

1. The States Parties to the present Covenant recognize the right of everyone:

(*a*) To take part in cultural life;

(*b*) To enjoy the benefits of scientific progress and its applications;

(*c*) To benefit from the protection of the moral and material interests resulting from any scientific, literary or artistic production of which he is the author.

2. The steps to be taken by the States Parties to the present Covenant to achieve the full realization of this right shall include those necessary for the conservation, the development and the diffusion of science and culture.

3. The States Parties to the present Covenant undertake to respect the freedom indispensable for scientific research and creative activity.

4. The States Parties to the present Covenant recognize the benefits to be derived from the encouragement and development of international contacts and co-operation in the scientific and cultural fields.

PART IV
Article 16

1. The States Parties to the present Covenant undertake to submit in conformity with this part of the Covenant reports on the measures which they have adopted and the progress made in achieving the observance of the rights recognized herein.

2. (a) All reports shall be submitted to the Secretary-General of the United Nations who shall transmit copies to the Economic and Social Council for consideration in accordance with the provisions of the present Covenant.

(b) The Secretary-General of the United Nations shall also transmit to the specialized agencies copies of the reports, or any relevant parts therefrom, from States Parties to the present Covenant which are also members of these specialized agencies in so far as these reports, or parts therefrom, relate to any matters which fall within the responsibilities of the said agencies in accordance with their constitutional instruments.

Article 17

1. The States Parties to the present Covenant shall furnish their reports in stages, in accordance with a programme to be established by the Economic and Social Council within one year of the entry into force of the present Covenant after consultation with the States Parties and the specialized agencies concerned.

2. Reports may indicate factors and difficulties affecting the degree of fulfillment of obligations under the present Covenant.

3. Where relevant information has previously been furnished to the United Nations or to any specialized agency by any State Party to the present Covenant it will not be necessary to reproduce that information but a precise reference to the information so furnished will suffice.

Article 18

Pursuant to its responsibilities under the Charter in the field of human rights and fundamental freedoms, the Economic and Social Council may make arrangements with the specialized agencies in respect of their reporting to it on the progress made in achieving the observance of the provisions of the present Covenant falling within the scope of their activities. These reports may include particulars of decisions and recommendations on such implementation adopted by their competent organs.

Article 19

The Economic and Social Council may transmit to the Commission on Human Rights for study and general recommendation or as appropriate for information the reports concerning human rights submitted by States in accordance with articles 16 and 17, and those concerning human rights submitted by the specialized agencies in accordance with article 18.

Article 20

The States Parties to the present Covenant and the specialized agencies concerned may submit comments to the Economic and Social Council on any general recommendation under article 19 or reference to such general recommendation in any report on the Commission or any documentation referred to therein.

Article 21

The Economic and Social Council may submit from time to time to the General Assembly reports with recommendations of a general nature and a summary of the information received from the States Parties to the present Covenant and the specialized agencies on the measures taken and the progress made in achieving general observance of the rights recognized in the present Covenant.

Article 22

The Economic and Social Council may bring to the attention of other organs of the United Nations, their subsidiary organs and specialized agencies concerned with furnishing technical assistance, any matters arising out of the reports referred to in this part of the present Covenant which may assist such bodies in deciding each within its field of competence, on the advisability of international measures likely to contribute to the effective progressive implementation of the present Covenant.

Article 23

The States Parties to the present Covenant agree that international action for the achievement of the rights recognized in the present Covenant includes such methods as the conclusion of conventions, the adoption of recommendations, the furnishing of technical assistance and the holding of regional meetings and technical meetings for the purpose of consultation and study organized in conjunction with the Governments concerned.

Article 24

Nothing in the present Covenant shall be interpreted as impairing the provisions of the Charter of the United Nations and of the constitutions of the specialized agencies which define the respective responsibilities of the various organs of the United Nations and of the specialized agencies in regard to the matters dealt with in the present Covenant.

Article 25

Nothing in the present Covenant shall be interpreted as impairing the inherent right of all peoples to enjoy and utilize fully and freely their natural wealth and resouces.

PART V
Article 26

1. The present Covenant is open for signature by any State Member of the United Nations or member of any of its specialized agencies, by any State Party to the Statute of the International Court of Justice, and by any other State which has been invited by the General Assembly of the United Nations to become a party to the present Covenant.
2. The present Covenant is subject to ratification. Instruments of ratification shall be deposited with the Secretary-General of the United Nations.
3. The present Covenant shall be open to accession by any State referred to in paragraph 1 of this article.
4. Accession shall be effected by the deposit of an instrument of accession with the Secretary-General of the United Nations.
5. The Secretary-General of the United Nations shall inform all States which have signed the present Covenant or acceded to it of the deposit of each instrument of ratification or accession.

Article 27

1. The present Covenant shall enter into force three months after the date of the deposit with the Secretary-General of the United Nations of the thirty-fifth instrument of ratification or instrument of accession.
2. For each State ratifying the present Covenant or acceding to it after the deposit of the thirty-fifth instrument of ratification or instrument of accession, the present Covenant shall enter into force three months after the date of the deposit of its own instrument of ratification or instrument of accession.

Article 28

The provisions of the present Covenant shall extend to all parts of federal States without any limitations or exceptions.

Article 29

1. Any State Party to the present Covenant may propose an amendment and file it with the Secretary-General of the

United Nations. The Secretary-General of the United Nations shall thereupon communicate any proposed amendments to the States Parties to the present Covenant with a request that they notify him whether they favour a conference of States Parties for the purpose of considering and voting upon the proposal. In the event that at least one third of the States Parties favours such a conference the Secretary-General of the United Nations shall convene the conference under the auspices of the United Nations. Any amendment adopted by a majority of the States Parties present and voting at the conference shall be submitted to the General Assembly of the United Nations for approval.

2. Amendments shall come into force when they have been approved by the General Assembly and accepted by a two-thirds majority of the States Parties to the present Covenant in accordance with their respective constitutional processes.

3. When amendments come into force they shall be binding on those States Parties which have accepted them, other States Parties being still bound by the provisions of the present Convenant and any earlier amendment which they have accepted.

Article 30

Irrespective of the notifications made under article 26, paragraph 5, the Secretary-General of the United Nations shall inform all States referred to in paragraph 1 of the same article of the following particulars:

(*a*) Signatures, ratifications and accessions under article 26;

(*b*) The date of the entry into force of the present Covenant under article 27 and the date of the entry into force of any amendments under article 29.

Article 31

1. The present Covenant, of which the Chinese, English, French, Russian and Spanish texts are equally authentic, shall be deposited in the archives of the United Nations.

2. The Secretary-General of the United Nations shall transmit certified copies of the present Covenant to all States referred to in article 26.

International Covenant on Civil and Political Rights

*   *   *

Preamble

The States Parties to the present Covenant,

Considering that, in accordance with the principles proclaimed in the Charter of the United Nations, recognition of the inherent dignity and of the equal and inalienable rights of all members of the human family is the foundation of freedom, justice and peace in the world,

Recognizing that these rights derive from the inherent dignity of the human person,

Recognizing that, in accordance with the Universal Declaration of Human Rights, the ideal of free human beings enjoying civil and political freedom and freedom from fear and want can only be achieved if conditions are created whereby everyone may enjoy his civil and political rights, as well as his economic, social and cultural rights,

Considering the obligation of States under the Charter of the United Nations to promote universal respect for, and observance of, human rights and freedoms,

Realizing that the individual, having duties to other individuals and to the community to which he belongs, is under a responsibility to strive for the promotion and observance of the rights recognized in the present Covenant,

Agree upon the following articles:

PART I
Article 1

1. All peoples have the right of self-determination. By virtue of the right they freely determine their political status

and freely pursue their economic, social and cultural development.

2. All peoples may, for their own ends, freely dispose of their natural wealth and resources without prejudice to any obligations arising out of international economic co-operation, based upon the principle of mutual benefit, and international law. In no case may a people be deprived of its own means of subsistence.

3. The States Parties to the present Covenant, including those having responsibility for the administration of Non-Self-Governing and Trust Territories, shall promote the realization of the right of self-determination, and shall respect that right, in conformity with the provisions of the United Nations Charter.

PART II
Article 2

1. Each State Party to the present Covenant undertakes to respect and to ensure to all individuals within its territory and subject to its jurisdiction the rights recognized in the present Covenant, without distinction of any kind, such as race, colour, sex, language, religion, political or other opinion, national or social origin, property, birth or other status.

2. Where not already provided for by existing legislative or other measures, each State Party to the present Covenant undertakes to take the necessary steps, in accordance with its constitutional processes and with the provisions of the present Covenant, to adopt such legislative or other measures as may be necessary to give effect to the rights recognized in the present Covenant.

3. Each State Party to the present Covenant undertakes:

(*a*) To ensure that any person whose rights or freedoms as herein recognized are violated shall have an effective remedy notwithstanding that the violation has been committed by persons acting in an official capacity;

(*b*) To ensure that any person claiming such a remedy shall have his right thereto determined by competent judicial, administrative or legislative authorities, or by any other competent authority provided for by the legal system of the State, and to develop the possibilities of judicial remedy;

    (*c*) To ensure that the competent authorities shall enforce such remedies when granted.

Article 3

The States Parties to the present Covenant undertake to ensure the equal right of men and women to the enjoyment of all civil and political rights set forth in the present Covenant.

Article 4

1. In time of public emergency which threatens the life of the nation and the existence of which is officially proclaimed, the States Parties to the present Covenant may take measures derogating from their obligations under the present Covenant to the extent strictly required by the exigencies of the situation, provided that such measures are not inconsistent with their other obligations under international law and do not involve discrimination solely on the ground of race, colour, sex, language, religion or social origin.

2. No derogation from articles 6, 7, 8 (paragraphs 1 and 2), 11, 15, 16 and 18 may be made under this provision.

3. Any State Party to the present Covenant availing itself of the right of derogation shall inform immediately the other States Parties to the present Covenant, through the intermediary of the Secretary-General of the United Nations of the provisions from which it has derogated and of the reasons by which is was actuated. A further communication shall be made, through the same intermediary, on the date on which it terminates such derogation.

Article 5

1. Nothing in the present Covenant may be interpreted as implying for any State, group or person any right to engage in any activity or perform any act aimed at the destruction of any of the rights and freedoms recognized herein or

at their limitation to a greater extent than is provided for in the present Covenant.

2. There shall be no restriction upon or derogation from any of the fundamental human rights recognized or existing in any State Party to the present Covenant pursuant to law, conventions, regulations or custom on the pretext that the present Covenant does not recognize such rights or that it recognizes them to a lesser extent.

PART III
Article 6

1. Every human being has the inherent right to life. This right shall be protected by law. No one shall be arbitrarily deprived of his life.

2. In countries which have not abolished the death penalty, sentence of death may be imposed only for the most serious crimes in accordance with law in force at the time of the commission of the crime and not contrary to the provisions of the present Covenant and to the Convention on the Prevention and Punishment of the Crime of Genocide. This penalty can only be carried out pursuant to a final judgement rendered by a competent court.

3. When deprivation of life constitutes the crime of genocide, it is understood that nothing in this article shall authorize any State Party to the present Covenant to derogate in any way from any obligation assumed under the provisions of the Convention on the Prevention and Punishment of the Crime of Genocide.

4. Anyone sentenced to death shall have the right to seek pardon or commutation of the sentence. Amnesty, pardon or commutation of the sentence of death may be granted in all cases.

5. Sentence of death shall not be imposed for crimes committed by persons below eighteen years of age and shall not be carried out on pregnant women.

6. Nothing in this article shall be invoked to delay or to prevent the abolition of capital punishment by any State Party to the present Covenant.

Article 7

No one shall be subjected to torture or to cruel, inhuman or degrading treatment or punishment. In particular, no one shall be subjected without his free consent to medical or scientific experimentation.

Article 8

1. No one shall be held in slavery; slavery and the slave-trade in all their forms shall be prohibited.
2. No one shall be held in servitude.
3. (a) No one shall be required to perform forced or compulsory labour;

(b) The preceding sub-paragraph shall not be held to preclude in countries where imprisonment with hard labour may be imposed as a punishment for a crime, the performance of hard labour in pursuance of a sentence to such punishment by a competent court;

(c) For the purpose of this paragraph the term "forced or compulsory labour" shall not include:

(*i*) Any work or service, not referred to in sub-paragraph (b), normally required of a person who is under detention in consequence of a lawful order of a court, or of a person during conditional release from such detention;

(*ii*) Any service of a military character and, in countries where conscientious objection is recognized, any national service required by law of conscientious objectors;

(*iii*) Any service exacted in cases of emergency or calamity threatening the life or well-being of the community;

(*iv*) Any work or service which forms part of normal civil obligations.

Article 9

1. Everyone has the right to liberty and security of person. No one shall be subjected to arbitrary arrest or detention. No one shall be deprived of his liberty except on such grounds and in accordance with such procedures as are established by law.
2. Anyone who is arrested shall be informed, at the time

of arrest, of the reasons for his arrest and shall be promptly informed of any charges against him.

3. Anyone arrested or detained on a criminal charge shall be brought promptly before a judge or other officer authorized by law to exercise judicial power and shall be entitled to trial within a reasonable time or to release. It shall not be the general rule that persons awaiting trial shall be detained in custody, but release may be subject to guarantees to appear for trial, at any other stage of the judicial proceedings, and, should occasion arise, for execution of the judgement.

4. Anyone who is deprived of his liberty by arrest or detention shall be entitled to take proceedings before a court, in order that such court may decide without delay on the lawfulness of his detention and order his release if the detention is not lawful.

5. Anyone who has been the victim of unlawful arrest or detention shall have an enforceable right to compensation.

Article 10

1. All persons deprived of their liberty shall be treated with humanity and with respect for the inherent dignity of the human person.

2. (a) Accused persons shall, save in exceptional circumstances, be segregated from convicted persons, and shall be subject to separate treatment appropriate to their status as unconvicted persons:

(b) Accused juvenile persons shall be separated from adults and brought as speedily as possible for adjudication.

3. The penitentiary system shall comprise treatment of prisoners the essential aim of which shall be their reformation and social rehabilitation. Juvenile offenders shall be segregated from adults and be accorded treatment appropriate to their age and legal status.

Article 11

No one shall be imprisoned merely on the ground of inability to fulfill a contractual obligation.

Article 12

1. Everyone lawfully within the territory of a State shall, within that territory, have the right to liberty of movement and freedom to choose his residence.
2. Everyone shall be free to leave any country, including his own.
3. The above-mentioned rights shall not be subject to any restrictions except those which are provided by law, are necessary to protect national security, public order (*"ordre public"*), public health or morals or the rights and freedoms of others, and are consistent with the other rights recognized in the present Covenant.
4. No one shall be arbitrarily deprived of the right to enter his own country.

Article 13

An alien lawfully in the territory of a State Party to the present Covenant may be expelled therefrom only in pursuance of a decision reached in accordance with law and shall, except where compelling reasons of national security otherwise require, be allowed to submit the reasons against his expulsion and to have his case reviewed by, and be represented for the purpose before, the competent authority or a person or persons especially designated by the competent authority.

Article 14

1. All persons shall be equal before the courts and tribunals. In the determination of any criminal charge against him, or his rights and obligations in a suit at law, everyone shall be entitled to a fair and public hearing by a competent, independent and impartial tribunal established by law. The Press and the public may be excluded from all or part of a trial for reasons of morals, public order (*"ordre public"*) or national security in a democratic society, or when the interest of the private lives of the parties so requires, or to the extent strictly necessary in the opinion of the court in special circumstances where publicity would prejudice the interests of justice; but

any judgment rendered in a criminal case or in a suit at law shall be made public except where the interest of juveniles otherwise requires or the proceedings concern matrimonial disputes or the guardianship of children.

2. Everyone charged with a criminal offence shall have the right to be presumed innocent until proved guilty according to law.

3. In the determination of any criminal charge against him, everyone shall be entitled to the following minimum guarantees, in full equality:

(*a*) To be informed promptly and in detail in a language which he understands of the nature and cause of the charges against him;

(*b*) To have adequate time and facilities for the preparation of his defence and to communicate with counsel of his own choosing;

(*c*) To be tried without undue delay;

(*d*) To be tried in his presence, and to defend himself in person or through legal assistance of his own choosing; to be informed, if he does not have legal assistance, of this right; and to have legal assistance assigned to him, in any case where the interests of justice so require, and without payment by him in any such case if he does not have sufficient means to pay for it;

(*e*) To examine, or have examined, the witnesses against him and to obtain the attendance and examination of witnesses on his behalf under the same conditions as witnesses against him;

(*f*) To have the free assistance of an interpreter if he cannot understand or speak the language used in court;

(*g*) Not to be compelled to testify against himself, or to confess guilt.

4. In the case of juveniles, the procedure shall be such as will take account of their age and the desirability of promoting their rehabilitation.

5. Everyone convicted of a crime shall have the right to his conviction and sentence being reviewed by a higher tribunal according to law.

6. When a person has by a final decision been convicted

of a criminal offence and when subsequently his conviction has been reversed or he has been pardoned on the ground that a new or newly discovered fact shows conclusively that there has been a miscarriage of justice, the person who has suffered punishment as a result of such conviction shall be compensated according to law, unless it is proved that the non-disclosure of the unknown fact in time is wholly or partly attributable to him.

7. No one shall be liable to be tried or punished again for an offence for which he has already been finally convicted or acquitted in accordance with the law and penal procedure of each country.

Article 15

1. No one shall be held guilty of any criminal offence on account of any act or omission which did not constitute a criminal offence, under national or international law, at the time when it was committed. Nor shall a heavier penalty be imposed than the one that was applicable at the time when the criminal offence was committed. If, subsequently to the commission of the offence, provision is made by law for the imposition of a lighter penalty, the offender shall benefit thereby.

2. Nothing in this article shall prejudice the trial and punishment of any person for any act or omission which, at the time when it was committed, was criminal according to the general principles of law recognized by the community of nations.

Article 16

Everyone shall have the right to recognition everywhere as a person before the law.

Article 17

1. No one shall be subjected to arbitrary or unlawful interference with his privacy, family, home or correspondence, nor to unlawful attacks on his honour and reputation.

2. Everyone has the right to the protection of the law against such interference or attacks.

Article 18

1. Everyone shall have the right to freedom of thought, conscience and religion. This right shall include freedom to have or to adopt a religion or belief of his choice, and freedom either individually or in community with others and in public or private, to manifest his religion or belief in worship, observance, practice and teaching.

2. No one shall be subject to coercion which would impair his freedom to have or to adopt a religion or belief of his choice.

3. Freedom to manifest one's religion or beliefs may be subject only to such limitations as are prescribed by law and are necessary to protect public safety, order, health, or morals or the fundamental rights and freedoms of others.

4. The States Parties to the present Covenant undertake to have respect for the liberty of parents and, when applicable, legal guardians, to ensure the religious and moral education of their children in conformity with their own convictions.

Article 19

1. Everyone shall have the right to hold opinions without interference.

2. Everyone shall have the right to freedom of expression; this right shall include freedom to seek, receive and impart information and ideas of all kinds, regardless of frontiers, either orally, in writing or in print, in the form of art, or through any other media of his choice.

3. The exercise of the rights provided for in the foregoing paragraph carries with it special duties and responsibilities. It may therefore be subject to certain restrictions, but these shall be such only as are provided by law and are necessary, (1) for respect of the rights or reputations of others, (2) for the protection of national security or of public order ("*ordre public*"), or of public health or morals.

Article 20

1. Any propaganda for war shall be prohibited by law.

2. Any advocacy of national, racial, or religious hatred that constitutes incitement to discrimination, hostility or violence shall be prohibited by law.

Article 21

The right of peaceful assembly shall be recognized. No restrictions may be placed on the exercise of this right other than those imposed in conformity with the law and which are necessary in a democratic society in the interests of national security or public safety, public order (*"ordre public"*), the protection of public health or morals or the protection of the rights and freedoms of others.

Article 22

1. Everyone shall have the right to freedom of association with others, including the right to form and join trade unions for the protection of his interests.
2. No restrictions may be placed on the exercise of this right other than those prescribed by law and which are necessary in a democratic society in the interests of national security or public safety, public order (*"ordre public"*), the protection of public health or morals or the protection of the rights and freedoms of others. This article shall not prevent the imposition of lawful restrictions on members of the armed forces and of the policy in their exercise of this right.
3. Nothing in this article shall authorize States Parties to the International Labour Convention of 1948 on Freedom of Association and Protection of the Right to Organise to take legislative measures which would prejudice, or to apply the law in such a manner as to prejudice, the guarantees provided for in the Convention.

Article 23

1. The family is the natural and fundamental group unit of society and is entitled to protection by society and the State.
2. The right of men and women of marriageable age to marry and to found a family shall be recognized.

3. No marriage shall be entered into without the free and full consent of the intending spouses.

4. States Parties to the present Covenant shall take appropriate steps to ensure equality of rights and responsibilities of spouses as to marriage, during marriage and at its dissolution. In the case of disolution, provision shall be made for the necessary protection of any children.

Article 24

1. Every child shall have, without any discrimination as to race, colour, sex, language, religion, national or social origin, property or birth, the right to such measures of protection as required by his status as a minor, on the part of his family, the society and the State.

2. Every child shall be registered immediately after birth and shall have a name.

3. Every child has the right to acquire a nationality.

Article 25

Every citizen shall have the right and the opportunity, without any of the distinctions mentioned in article 2 and without unreasonable restrictions:

(*a*) To take part in the conduct of public affairs, directly or through freely chosen representatives;

(*b*) To vote and to be elected at genuine periodic elections which shall be by universal and equal suffrage and shall be held by secret ballot, guaranteeing the free expression of the will of the electors;

(*c*) To have access, on general terms of equality, to public service in his country.

Article 26

All persons are equal before the law and are entitled without any discrimination to equal protection of the law. In this respect the law shall prohibit any discrimination and guarantee to all persons equal and effective protection against discrimination on any ground such as race, colour, sex, language, religion, political or other opinion, national or social origin, property, birth or other status.

Article 27

In those States in which ethnic, religious or linguistic minorities exist, persons belonging to such minorities shall not be denied the right, in community with the other members of their group, to enjoy their own culture, to profess and practice their own religion, or to use their own language.

PART IV
Article 28

1. There shall be established in a Human Rights Committee (hereafter referred to in the present Covenant as "the Committee"). It shall consist of eighteen members and shall carry out the functions hereinafter provided.

2. The Committee shall be composed of nationals of the States Parties to the present Covenant who shall be persons of high moral character and recognized competence in the field of human rights, consideration being given to the usefulness of the participation of some persons having legal experience.

3. The members of the Committee shall be elected and shall serve in their personal capacity.

Article 29

1. The members of the Committee shall be elected by secret ballot from a list of persons possessing the qualifications prescribed in article 28 and nominated for the purpose by the States Parties to the present Covenant.

2. Each State Party to the present Covenant may nominate not more than two persons. These persons shall be nationals of the nominating State.

3. A person shall be eligible for renomination.

Article 30

1. The initial election shall be held no later than six months after the date of the entry into force of the present Covenant.

2. At least four months before the date of each election of the Committee, other than an election to fill a vacancy declared in accordance with article 34, the Secretary-General

of the United Nations shall address a written invitation to
the States Parties to the present Covenant to submit their
nominations for membership of the Committee within three
months.

3. The Secretary-General of the United Nations shall prepare a list in alphabetical order of all the persons thus nominated, with an indication of the States Parties which have
nominated them, and shall submit it to the States Parties to
the present Covenant no later than one month before the
date of each election.

4. Elections of the members of the Committee shall be
held at a meeting of the States Parties to the present Covenant convened by the Secretary-General of the United Nations at the Headquarters of the United Nations. At that
meeting, for which two thirds of the States Parties to the
present Covenant shall constitute a quorum, the persons
elected to the Committee shall be those nominees who obtain
the largest number of votes and an absolute majority of the
votes of the representatives of States Parties present and voting.

Article 31

1. The Committee may not include more than one national of the same state.

2. In the election of tbe Committee consideration shall be
given to equitable geographical distribution of membership
and to the representation of the different forms of civilization as well as of the principal legal systems.

Article 32

1. The members of the Committee shall be elected for a
term of four years. They shall be eligible for re-election if
renominated. However, the terms of nine of the members
elected at the first election shall expire at the end of two
years, immediately after the first election the names of these
nine members shall be chosen by lot by the Chairman of the
meeting referred to in paragraph 4 of article 30.

2. Elections at the expiry of office shall be held in accordance with the preceding articles of this part of the present
Covenant.

Article 33

1. If, in the unanimous opinion of the other members, a member of the Committee has ceased to carry out his functions for any cause other than absence of a temporary character, the Chairman of the Committee shall notify the Secretary-General of the United Nations who shall then declare the seat of that member to be vacant.

2. In the event of the death or the resignation of a member of the Committee, the Chairman shall immediately notify the Secretary-General of the United Nations who shall declare the seat vacant from the date of death or the date on which the resignation takes effect.

Article 34

1. When a vacancy is declared in accordance with article 33 and if the term of office of the member to be replaced does not expire within six months of the declaration of the vacancy, the Secretary-General of the United Nations shall notify each of the States Parties to the present Covenant which may within two months submit nominations in accordance with article 29 for the purpose of filling the vacancy.

2. The Secretary-General of the United Nations shall prepare a list in alphabetical order of the persons thus nominated and shall submit it to the States Parties to the present Covenant. The election to fill the vacancy shall then take place in accordance with the relevant provisions of this part of the present Covenant.

3. A member of the Committee elected to fill a vacancy declared in accordance with article 33 shall hold office for the remainder of the term of the member who vacated the seat on the Committee under the provisions of that article.

Article 35

The members of the Committee shall, with the approval of the General Assembly of the United Nations, receive emoluments from United Nations resources on such terms and conditions as the General Assembly may decide having regard to the importance of the Committee's responsibilities.

Article 36

The Secretary-General of the United Nations shall provide the necessary staff and facilities for the effective performance of the functions of the Committee under this Covenant.

Article 37

1. The Secretary-General of the United Nations shall convene the initial meeting of the Committee at the Headquarters of the United Nations.
2. After its initial meeting, the Committee shall meet at such times as shall be provided in its rules of procedure.
3. The Committee shall normally meet at the Headquarters of the United Nations or at the United Nations Office at Geneva.

Article 38

Every member of the Committee shall, before taking up his duties, make a solemn declaration in open committee that he will perform his functions impartially and conscientiously.

Article 39

1. The Committee shall elect its officers for a term of two years. They may be re-elected.
2. The Committee shall establish its own rules of procedure, but these rules shall provide, *inter alia*, that:
    (*a*) Twelve members shall constitute a quorum;
    (*b*) Decisions of the Committee shall be made by a majority vote of the members present.

Article 40

1. The States Parties to the present Covenant undertake to submit reports on the measures they have adopted which give effect to the rights recognized herein and on the progress made in the enjoyment of those rights; (a) within one year of the entry into force of the present Covenant for the States Parties concerned and (b) thereafter whenever the Committee so requests.

2. All reports shall be submitted to the Secretary-General of the United Nations who shall transmit them to the Committee for consideration. Reports shall indicate the factors and difficulties, if any, affecting the implementation of the present Covenant.

3. The Secretary-General of the United Nations may after consultation with the Committee transmit to the specialized agencies concerned copies of such parts of the reports as may fall within their field of competence.

4. The Committee shall study the reports submitted by the States Parties to the present Covenant. It shall transmit its reports and such general comments as it may consider appropriate to the States Parties. The Committee may also transmit to the Economic and Social Council these comments along with the copies of the reports it has received from States Parties to the present Covenant.

5. The States Parties to the present Covenant may submit to the Committee observations on any comments that may be made in accordance with paragraph 4 of this article.

Article 41

1. A State Party to the present Covenant may at any time declare under this article that it recognizes the competence of the Committee to receive and consider communications to the effect that a State Party claims that another State Party is not fulfilling its obligations under the present Covenant. Communications under this article may be received and considered only if submitted by a State Party which has made a declaration recognizing in regard to itself the competence of the Committee. No communication shall be received by the Committee if it concerns a State Party which has not made such a declaration. Communications received under this article shall be dealt with in accordance with the following procedure:

(a) If a State Party to the present Covenant considers that another State Party is not giving effect to the provisions of the present Covenant, it may, by written communication, bring the matter to the attention of that State Party. Within three months after the receipt of the communication, the receiving State shall afford the State which sent the communication an explanation or any other statement in writing clarifying the matter, which should include, to the extent possible and pertinent, reference to domestic procedures and remedies taken, pending, or available in the matter.

(b) If the matter is not adjusted to the satisfaction of both States Parties concerned within six months after the receipt by the receiving State of the initial communication, either State shall have the right to refer the matter to the Committee, by notice given to the Committee and to the other State.

(c) The Committee shall deal with a matter referred to it only after it has ascertained that all available domestic remedies have been invoked and exhausted in the matter, in conformity with the generally recognized principles of international law. This shall not be the rule where the application of the remedies is unreasonably prolonged.

(d) The Committee shall hold closed meetings when examining communications under this article.

(e) Subject to the provisions of sub-paragraph (c), the Committee shall make available its good offices to the States Parties concerned with a view to a friendly solution of the matter on the basis of respect for human rights and fundamental freedoms as recognized in this Covenant.

(f) In any matter referred to it, the Committee may call upon the States Parties concerned, referred to in sub-paragraph (b), to supply any relevant information.

(g) The States Parties concerned, referred to in sub-paragraph (b), shall have the right to be represented when the matter is being considered in the Committee and to make submissions orally and/or in writing.

(h) The Committee shall, within twelve months after the date of receipt of notice under sub-paragraph (b), submit a report:

(*i*) If a solution within the terms of sub-paragraph (e) is reached, the Committee shall confine its report to a brief statement of the facts and of the solution reached;

(*ii*) If a solution is not reached, within the terms of sub-paragraph (e), the Committee shall confine its report to a brief statement of the facts; the written submissions and record of the oral submissions made by the States Parties concerned shall be attached to the report.

In every matter the report shall be communicated to the States Parties concerned.

2. The provisions of this article shall come into force when ten States Parties to the present Covenant have made declarations under paragraph 1 of this article. Such declarations shall be deposited by the States Parties with the Secretary-General of the United Nations who shall transmit copies thereof to the other States Parties. A declaration may be withdrawn at any time by notification to tbe Secretary-General. Such a withdrawal shall not prejudice the consideration of any matter which is the subject of a communication already transmitted under this article; no further communication by any State Party shall be received after the notification of withdrawal of the declaration has been received by the Secretary-General of the United Nations unless the State Party concerned had made a new declaration.

Article 42

1. (a) If a matter referred to the Committee in accordance with article 41 is not resolved to the satisfaction of the States Parties concerned, the Committee may, with the prior consent of the States Parties concerned, appoint an *ad hoc* Conciliation Commission (hereinafter referred to as "the Commission"). The good offices of the Commission shall be made available to the States Parties concerned with a view to an amicable solution of the matter on the basis of respect for the present Covenant;

(b) The Commission shall consist of five persons acceptable to the States Parties concerned. If the States Parties concerned fail to reach agreement within three months on all or part of the composition of the Commission the members of the Commission concerning whom no agreement was reached shall be selected by secret ballot by a two-thirds majority vote of the Committee from among its members.

2. The members of the Commission shall serve in their personal capacity. They shall not be nationals of the States Parties concerned, or of a State not party to the present Covenant, or of a State Party which has not made a declaration under article 41.

3. The Commission shall elect its own Chairman and adopt its own rules of procedure.

4. The meetings of the Commission shall normally be held at the Headquarters of the United Nations or at the United Nations Office at Geneva. However, they may be held at such other convenient places as the Commission may determine in consultation with the Secretary-General of the United Nations and the States Parties concerned.

5. The secretariat provided in accordance with article 36 shall also service the Commissions appointed under this article.

6. The information received and collated by the Committee shall be made available to the Commission and the Commission may call upon the States Parties concerned to supply any other relevant information.

7. When the Commission has fully considered the matter, but in any event not later than twelve months after having been seized of the matter, it shall submit to the Chairman of the Committee a report for communication of the States Parties concerned.

(a) If the Commission is unable to complete its consideration of the matter within twelve months, it shall confine its report to a brief statement of the status of its consideration of the matter.

(b) If an amicable solution of the matter on the basis of respect for human rights as recognized in the present Covenant is reached, the Commission shall confine its report to a brief statement of the facts and of the solution reached.

(c) If a solution within the terms of sub-paragraph (b) is not reached, the Commission's report shall embody its findings on all questions of fact relevant to the issues between the States Parties concerned, as well as its views on the possibilities of amicable solution of the matter. This report shall also contain the written submissions and a record of the oral submissions made by the States Parties concerned.

(d) If the Commission's report is submitted under sub-paragraph (c), the States Parties concerned shall, within three months of the receipt of the report, inform the Chairman of the Committee whether or not they accept the contents of the report of the Commission.

8. The provisions of this article are without prejudice to the responsibilities of the Committee under article 41.

9. The States Parties concerned shall share equally all the expenses of the members of the Commission in accordance with estimates to be provided by the Secretary-General of the United Nations.

10. The Secretary-General of the United Nations shall be empowered to pay the expenses of the members of the Commission, if necessary, before reimbursement by the States Parties concerned in accordance with paragraph 9 of this article.

Article 43

The members of the Committee and of the *ad hoc* conciliation commissions which may be appointed under article 41, shall be entitled to the facilities, privileges and immunities of experts on mission for the United Nations as laid down in the relevant sections of the Convention on the Privileges and Immunities of the United Nations.

Article 44

The provisions for the implementation of the present Covenant shall apply without prejudice to the procedures prescribed in the field of human rights by or under the constituent instruments and the conventions of the United Nations and of the specialized agencies and shall not prevent the States Parties to the present Covenant from having recourse to other procedures for settling a dispute in accordance with general or special international agreements in force between them.

Article 45

The Committee shall submit to the General Assembly, through the Economic and Social Council, an annual report on its activities.

PART V
Article 46

Nothing in the present Covenant shall be interpreted as impairing the provisions of the Charter of the United Nations and of the constitutions of the specialized agencies which define the respective responsibilities of the various organs of the United Nations and of the specialized agencies in regard to the matters dealt with in the present Covenant.

Article 47

Nothing in the Covenant shall be interpreted as impairing the inherent right of all peoples to enjoy and utilize fully and freely their natural wealth and resources.

PART VI
Article 48

1. The present Covenant is open for signature by any State Member of the United Nations or members of any of is specialized agencies, by any State Party to the Statute of the International Court of Justice, and by any other State which has been invited by the General Assembly of the United Nations to become a party to the present Covenant.

2. The present Covenant is subject to ratification. Instruments of ratification shall be deposited with the Secretary-General of the United Nations.

3. The present Covenant shall be open to accession by any State referred to in paragraph 1 of this article.

4. Accession shall be effected by the deposit of an instrument of accession with the Secretary-General of the United Nations.

5. The Secretary-General of the United Nations shall inform all States which have signed this Covenant or acceded to it of the deposit of each instrument of ratification or accession.

Article 49

1. The present Covenant shall enter into force three months after the date of the deposit with the Secretary-Gen-

eral of the United Nations of the thirty-fifth instrument of ratification or instrument of accession.

2. For each State ratifying the present Covenant or acceding to it after the deposit of the thirty-fifth instrument of ratification or instrument of accession, the present Covenant shall enter into force three months after the date of the deposit of its own instrument of ratification or instrument of accession.

Article 50

The provisions of the present Covenant shall extend to all parts of federal States without any limitations or exceptions.

Article 51

1. Any State Party to the present Covenant may propose an amendment and file it with the Secretary-General of the United Nations. The Secretary-General of the United Nations shall thereupon communicate any proposed amendments to the States Parties to the present Covenant with a request that they notify him whether they favour a conference of States Parties for the purpose of considering and voting upon the proposal. In the event that at least one third of the States Parties favours such a conference the Secretary-General of the United Nations shall convene the conference under the auspices of the United Nations. Any amendment adopted by a majority of the States Parties present and voting at the conference shall be submitted to the General Assembly of the United Nations for approval.

2. Amendments shall come into force when they have been approved by the General Assembly and accepted by a two-thirds majority of the States Parties to the Present Covenant in accordance with their respective constitutional processes.

3. When amendments come into force they shall be binding on those States Parties which have accepted them, other States Parties being still bound by the provisions of the present Covenant and any earlier amendment which they have accepted.

Article 52

Irrespective of the notifications made under article 48, paragraph 5, the Secretary-General of the United Nations shall inform all States referred to in paragraph 1 of the same article of the following particulars:

(*a*) Signatures, ratifications and accessions under article 48;

(*b*) The date of the entry into force of the present Covenant under article 49 and the date of the entry into force of any amendments under article 51.

Article 53

1. The present Covenant, of which the Chinese, English, French, Russian and Spanish texts are equally authentic, shall be deposited in the archives of the United Nations.

2. The Secretary-General of the United Nations shall transmit certified copies of the present Covenant to all States referred to in article 48.

American Convention on Human Rights "Pact of San Jose, Costa Rica"

*   *   *

Preamble

The American states signatory to the present Convention,

Reaffirming their intention to consolidate in this hemisphere, within the framework of democratic institutions, a system of personal liberty and social justice based on respect for the essential rights of man;

Recognizing that the essential rights of man are not derived from one's being a national of a certain state, but are based upon attributes of the human personality, and that they therefore justify international protection in the form of a convention reinforcing or complementing the protection provided by the domestic law of the American states;

Considering that these principles have been set forth in the Charter of the Organization of American States, in the American Declaration of the Rights and Duties of Man, and in the Universal Declaration of Human Rights, and that they have been reaffirmed and refined in other international instruments, worldwide as well as regional in scope;

Reiterating that, in accordance with the Universal Declaration of Human Rights, the ideal of free men enjoying freedom from fear and want can be achieved only if conditions are created whereby everyone may enjoy his economic, social, and cultural rights, as well as his civil and political rights; and

Considering that the Third Special Inter-American Conference (Buenos Aires, 1967) approved the incorporation into the Charter of the Organization itself of broader standards with respect to economic, social, and educational rights and resolved that an inter-American convention on human rights should determine the structure, competence, and procedure of the organs responsible for these matters,

Have agreed upon the following:

PART I—STATE OBLIGATIONS AND RIGHTS PROTECTED

CHAPTER I—GENERAL OBLIGATIONS

Article 1. Obligation to Respect Rights

1. The States Parties to this Convention undertake to respect the rights and freedoms recognized herein and to ensure to all persons subject to their jurisdiction the free and full exercise of those rights and freedoms, without any discrimination for reasons of race, color, sex, language, religion, political or other opinion, national or social origin, economic status, birth, or any other social condition.

2. For the purposes of this Convention, "person" means every human being.

Article 2. Domestic Legal Effects

Where the exercise of any of the rights or freedoms referred to in Article 1 is not already ensured by legislative or other provisions, the States Parties undertake to adopt, in accordance with their constituional processes and the provisions of this Convention, such legislative or other measures as may be necessary to give effect to those rights or freedoms.

CHAPTER II—CIVIL AND POLITICAL RIGHTS

Article 3. Right to Juridical Personality

Every person has the right to recognition as a person before the law.

Article 4. Right to Life

1. Every person has the right to have his life respected. This right shall be protected by law and, in general, from the moment of conception. No one shall be arbitrarily deprived of his life.

2. In countries that have not abolished the death penalty,

it may be imposed only for the most serious crimes and pursuant to a final judgment rendered by a competent court and in accordance with a law establishing such punishment, enacted prior to the commission of the crime. The application of such punishment shall not be extended to crimes to which it does not presently apply.

3. The death penalty shall not be reestablished in states that have abolished it.

4. In no case shall capital punishment be inflicted for political offenses or related common crimes.

5. Capital punishment shall not be imposed upon persons who, at the time the crime was committed, were under 18 years of age or over 70 years of age; nor shall it be applied to pregnant women.

6. Every person condemned to death shall have the right to apply for amnesty, pardon, or commutation of sentence, which may be granted in all cases. Capital punishment shall not be imposed while such a petition is pending decision by the competent authority.

Article 5. Right to Humane Treatment

1. Every person has the right to have his physical, mental, and moral integrity respected.

2. No one shall be subjected to torture or to cruel, inhuman, or degrading punishment or treatment. All persons deprived of their liberty shall be treated with respect for the inherent dignity of the human person.

3. Punishment shall not be extended to any person other than the criminal.

4. Accused persons shall, save in exceptional circumstances, be segregated from convicted persons, and shall be subject to separate treatment appropriate to their status as unconvicted persons.

5. Minors while subject to criminal proceedings shall be separated from adults and brought before specialized tribunals, as speedily as possible, so that they may be treated in accordance with their status as minors.

6. Punishments consisting of deprivation of liberty shall have as an essential aim the reform and social readaptation of the prisoners.

Article 6. *Freedom of Slavery*

1. No one shall be subject to slavery or to involuntary servitude, which are prohibited in all their forms, as are the slave trade and traffic in women.

2. No one shall be required to perform forced or compulsory labor. This provision shall not be interpreted to mean that, in those countries in which the penalty established for certain crimes is deprivation of liberty at forced labor, the carrying out of such a sentence imposed by a competent court is prohibited. Forced labor shall not adversely affect the dignity or the physical or intellectual capacity of the prisoner.

3. For the purposes of this article, the following do not constitute forced or compulsory labor:

(*a*) work or service normally required of a person imprisoned in execution of a sentence or formal decision passed by the competent judicial authority. Such work or service shall be carried out under the supervision and control of public authorities, and any persons performing such work or services shall not be placed at the disposal of any private party, company, or juridical person;

(*b*) military service and, in countries in which conscientious objectors are recognized, national service that the law may provide for in lieu of military service;

(*c*) service exacted in time of danger or calamity that threatens the existence or the well-being of the community; or

(*d*) work or service that forms part of normal civic obligations.

Article 7. *Right to Personal Liberty*

1. Every person has the right to personal liberty and security.

2. No one shall be deprived of his physical liberty except for the reasons and under the conditions established beforehand by the constitution of the State Party concerned or by a law established purusant thereto.

3. No one shall be subject to arbitrary arrest or imprisonment.

4. Anyone who is detained shall be informed of the reasons for his detention and shall be promptly notified of the charge or charges against him.

5. Any person detained shall be brought promptly before a judge or other officer authorized by law to exercise judicial power and shall be entitled to trial within a reasonable time or to be released without prejudice to the continuation of the proceedings. His release may be subject to guarantees to assure his appearance for trial.

6. Anyone who is deprived of his liberty shall be entitled to recourse to a competent court, in order that the court may decide without delay on the lawfulness of his arrest or detention and order his release if the arrest or detention is unlawful. In States Parties whose laws provide that anyone who believes himself to be threatened with deprivation of his liberty is entitled to recourse to a competent court in order that it may decide on the lawfulness of such threat, this remedy may not be restricted or abolished. The interested party or another person in his behalf is entitled to seek these remedies.

7. No one shall be detained for debt. This principle shall not limit the orders of a competent judicial authority issued for nonfulfillment of duties of support.

Article 8. Right to a Fair Trial

1. Every person has the right to a hearing, with due guarantees and within a reasonable time, by a competent, independent, and impartial tribunal, previously established by law, in the substantiation of any accusation of a criminal nature made against him or for the determination of his rights and obligations of a civil, labor, fiscal, or any other nature.

2. Every person accused of a criminal offense has the right to be presumed innocent so long as his guilt has not been proven according to law. During the proceedings, every person is entitled, with full equality, to the following minimum guarantees:

(a) the right of the accused to be assisted without charge by a translator or interpreter, if he does not understand or does not speak the language of the tribunal or court;

(*b*) prior notification in detail to the accused of the charges against him;

(*c*) adequate time and means for the preparation of his defense;

(*d*) the right of the accused to defend himself personally or to be assisted by legal counsel of his own choosing, and to communicate freely and privately with his counsel;

(*e*) the inalienable right to be assisted by counsel provided by the state, paid or not as the domestic law provides, if the accused does not defend himself personally or engage his own counsel within the time period established by law;

(*f*) the right of the defense to examine witnesses present in the court and to obtain the appearance, as witnesses, of experts or other persons who may throw light on the facts;

(*g*) the right not to be compelled to be a witness against himself or to plead guilty; and

(*h*) the right to appeal the judgment to a higher court.

3. A confession of guilt by the accused shall be valid only if it is made without coercion of any kind.

4. An accused person acquitted by a nonappealable judgment shall not be subjected to a new trial for the same cause.

5. Criminal proceedings shall be public, except insofar as may be necessary to protect the interests of justice.

Article 9. Freedom from Ex Post Facto Laws

No one shall be convicted of any act or omission that did not constitute a criminal offense, under the applicable law, at the time it was committed. A heavier penalty shall not be imposed than the one that was applicable at the time the criminal offense was committed. If subsequent to the commission of the offense the law provides for the imposition of a lighter punishment, the guilty person shall benefit therefrom.

Article 10. Right to Compensation

Every person has the right to be compensated in accordance with the law in the event he has been sentenced by a final judgment through a miscarriage of justice.

Article 11. Right to Privacy

1. Everyone has the right to have his honor respected and his dignity recognized.

2. No one may be the object of arbitrary or abusive interference with his private life, his family, his home, or his correspondence, or of unlawful attacks on his honor or reputation.

3. Everyone has the right to the protection of the law against such interference or attacks.

Article 12. Freedom of Conscience and Religion

1. Everyone has the right to freedom of conscience and of religion. This right includes freedom to maintain or to change one's religion or beliefs, and freedom to profess or disseminate one's religion or beliefs, either individually or together with others, in public or in private.

2. No one shall be subject to restrictions that might impair his freedom to maintain or to change his religion or beliefs.

3. Freedom to manifest one's religion and beliefs may be subject only to the limitations prescribed by law that are necessary to protect public safety, order, health, or morals, or the rights or freedoms of others.

4. Parents or guardians, as the case may be, have the right to provide for the religious and moral education of their children or wards that is in accord with their own convictions.

Article 13. Freedom of Thought and Expression

1. Everyone has the right to freedom of thought and expression. This right includes freedom to seek, receive, and impart information and ideas of all kinds, regardless of frontiers, either orally, in writing, in print, in the form of art, or through any other medium of one's choice.

2. The exercise of the right provided for in the foregoing paragraph shall not be subject to prior censorship but shall be subject to subsequent imposition of liability, which shall be expressly established by law to the extent necessary to ensure:

(*a*) respect for the rights or reputations of others; or

(*b*) the protection of national security, public order, or public health or morals.

3. The right of expression may not be restricted by indirect methods or means, such as the abuse of government or private controls over newsprint, radio broadcasting frequencies, or equipment used in the dissemination of information, or by any other means tending to impede the communication and circulation of ideas and opinions.

4. Notwithstanding the provisions of paragraph 2 above, public entertainments may be subject by law to prior censorship for the sole purpose of regulating access to them for the moral protection of childhood and adolescence.

5. Any propaganda for war and any advocacy of national, racial, or religious hatred that constitute incitements to lawless violence or to any other similar illegal action against any person or group of persons on any grounds including those of race, color, religion, language, or national origin shall be considered as offenses punishable by law.

Article 14. Right of Reply

1. Anyone injured by inaccurate or offensive statements or ideas disseminated to the public in general by a legally regulated medium of communication has the right to reply or to make a correction using the same communications outlet, under such conditions as the law may establish.

2. The correction or reply shall not in any case remit other legal liabilities that may have been incurred.

3. For the effective protection of honor and reputation, every publisher, and every newspaper, motion picture, radio, and television company, shall have a person responsible who is not protected by immunities or special privileges.

Article 15. Right of Assembly

The right of peaceful assembly, without arms, is recognized. No restrictions may be placed on the exercise of this right other than those imposed in conformity with the law and necessary in a democratic society in the interest of national security, public safety or public order, or to protect public health or morals or the rights or freedoms of others.

Article 16. Freedom of Association

1. Everyone has the right to associate freely for ideological, religious, political, economic, labor, social, cultural, sports, or other purposes.

2. The exercise of this right shall be subject only to such restrictions established by law as may be necessary in a democratic society, in the interest of national security, public safety or public order, or to protect public health or morals or the rights and freedoms of others.

3. The provisions of this article do not bar the imposition of legal restrictions, including even deprivation of the exercise of the right of association, on members of the armed forces and the police.

Article 17. Rights of the Family

1. The family is the natural and fundamental group unit of society and is entitled to protection by society and the state.

2. The right of men and women of marriageable age to marry and to raise a family shall be recognized, if they meet the conditions required by domestic laws, insofar as such conditions do not affect the principle of nondiscrimination established in this Convention.

3. No marriage shall be entered into without the free and full consent of the intending spouse.

4. The States Parties shall take appropriate steps to ensure the equality of rights and the adequate balancing of responsibilities of the spouses as to marriage, during marriage, and in the event of its dissolution. In case of dissolution, provision shall be made for the necessary protection of any children solely on the basis of their own best interests.

5. The law shall recognize equal rights for children born out of wedlock and those born in wedlock.

Article 18. Right to a Name

Every person has the right to a given name and to the surnames of his parents or that of one of them. The law shall regulate the manner in which this right shall be ensured for all, by the use of assumed names if necessary.

Article 19. Rights of the Child

Every minor child has the right to the measures of protection required by his condition as a minor on the part of his family, society, and the state.

Article 20. Right to Nationality

1. Every person has the right to a nationality.
2. Every person has the right to the nationality of the state in whose territory he was born if he does not have the right to any other nationality.
3. No one shall be arbitrarily deprived of his nationality or of the right to change it.

Article 21. Right to Property

1. Everyone has the right to the use and enjoyment of his property. The law may subordinate such use and enjoyment to the interest of society.
2. No one shall be deprived of his property except upon payment of just compensation, for reasons of public utility or social interest, and in the cases and according to the forms established by law.
3. Usury and any other form of exploitation of man by man shall be prohibited by law.

Article 22. Freedom of Movement and Residence

1. Every person lawfully in the territory of a State Party has the right to move about in it, and to reside in it subject to the provisions of the law.
2. Every person has the right to leave any country freely, including his own.
3. The exercise of the foregoing rights may be restricted only pursuant to a law to the extent necessary in a democratic society to prevent crime or to protect national security, public safety, public order, public morals, public health, or the rights or freedoms of others.
4. The exercise of the rights recognized in paragraph 1 may also be restricted by law in designated zones for reasons of public interest.
5. No one can be expelled from the territory of the state

of which he is a national or be deprived of the right to enter it.

6. An alien lawfully in the territory of a State Party to this Convention may be expelled from it only pursuant to a decision reached in accordance with law.

7. Every person has the right to seek and be granted asylum in a foreign territory, in accordance with the legislation of the state and international conventions, in the event he is being pursued for political offenses or related common crimes.

8. In no case may an alien be deported or returned to a country, regardless of whether or not it is his country of origin, if in that country his right to life or personal freedom is in danger of being violated because of his race, nationality, religion, social status, or political opinions.

9. The collective expulsion of aliens is prohibited.

Article 23. Right to Participate in Government

1. Every citizen shall enjoy the following rights and opportunities:

(*a*) to take part in the conduct of public affairs, directly or through freely chosen representatives;

(*b*) to vote and to be elected in genuine periodic elections, which shall be by universal and equal suffrage and by secret ballot that guarantees the free expression of the will of the voters; and

(*c*) to have access, under general conditions of equality, to the public service of his country.

2. The law may regulate the exercise of the rights and opportunities referred to in the preceding paragraph only on the basis of age, nationality, residence, language, education, civil and mental capacity, or sentencing by a competent court in criminal proceedings.

Article 24. Right to Equal Protection

All persons are equal before the law. Consequently, they are entitled, without discrimination, to equal protection of the law.

Article 25. *Right to Judicial Protection*

1. Everyone has the right to simple and prompt recourse, or any other effective recourse to a competent court or tribunal for protection against acts that violate his fundamental rights recognized by the constitution or laws of the state concerned or by this Convention, even though such violation may have been committed by persons acting in the course of their official duties.

2. The States Parties undertake:

(*a*) to ensure that any person claiming such remedy shall have his rights determined by the competent authority provided for by the legal system of the state;

(*b*) to develop the possibilities of judicial remedy; and

(*c*) to ensure that the competent authorities shall enforce such remedies when granted.

CHAPTER III—ECONOMIC, SOCIAL, AND CULTURAL RIGHTS

Article 26. *Progressive Development*

The States Parties undertake to adopt measures both internally and through international cooperation, especially those of an economic and technical nature, with a view to achieving progressively, by legislation or other appropriate means, the full realization of the rights implicit in the economic, social, educational, scientific, and cultural standards set forth in the Charter of the Organization of American States as amended by the Protocol of Buenos Aires.

CHAPTER IV—SUSPENSION OF GUARANTEES, INTERPRETATION, AND APPLICATION

Article 27. *Suspension of Guarantees*

1. In time of war, public danger, or other emergency that threatens the independence or security of a State Party, it may take measures derogating from its obligations under the present Convention to the extent and for the period of time strictly required by the exigencies of the situation, provided that such measures are not inconsistent with its other obligations under international law and do not involve discrimi-

nation on the ground of race, color, sex, language, religion, or social origin.

2. The foregoing provision does not authorize any suspension of the following articles: Article 3 (Right to Juridical Personality), Article 4 (Right to Life), Article 5 (Right to Humane Treatment), Article 6 (Freedom from Slavery), Article 9 (Freedom from *Ex Post Facto* Laws)), Article 12 (Freedom of Conscience and Religion), Article 17 (Rights of the Family), Article 18 (Right to a Name), Article 19 (Rights of the Child), Article 20 (Right to Nationality), and Article 23 (Right to Participate in Government), or of the judicial guarantees essential for the protection of such rights.

3. Any State Party availing itself of the right of suspension shall immediately inform the other States Parties, through the Secretary General of the Organization of American States, of the provisions the application of which it has suspended, the reasons that gave rise to the suspension, and the date set for the termination of such suspension.

Article 28. Federal Clause

1. Where a State Party is constituted as a federal state, the national government of such State Party shall implement all the provisions of the Convention over whose subject matter it exercises legislative and judicial jurisdiction.

2. With respect to the provisions over whose subject matter the constituent units of the federal state have jurisdiction, the national government shall immediately take suitable measures, in accordance with its constitution and its laws, to the end that the competent authorities of the constituent units may adopt appropriate provisions for the fulfillment of this Convention.

3. Whenever two or more States Parties agree to form a federation or other type of association, they shall take care that the resulting federal or other compact contains the provisions necessary for continuing and rendering effective the standards of this Convention in the new state that is organized.

Article 29. Restrictions Regarding Interpretation

No provision of this Convention shall be interpreted as:

(*a*) permitting any State Party, group, or person to suppress the enjoyment or exercise of the rights and freedoms recognized in this Convention or to restrict them to a greater extent than is provided for herein;

(*b*) restricting the enjoyment or exercise of any right or freedom recognized by virtue of the laws of any State Party or by virtue of another convention to which one of the said states is a party;

(*c*) precluding other rights or guarantees that are inherent in the human personality or derived from representative democracy as a form of government; or

(*d*) excluding or limiting the effect that the American Declaration of the Rights and Duties of Man and other international acts of the same nature may have.

Article 30. Scope of Restrictions

The restrictions that, pursuant to this Convention, may be placed on the enjoyment or exercise of the rights or freedoms recognized herein may not be applied except in accordance with laws enacted for reasons of general interest and in accordance with the purpose for which such restrictions have been established.

Article 31. Recognition of Other Rights

Other rights and freedoms recognized in accordance with the procedures established in Articles 76 and 77 may be included in the system of protection of this Convention.

CHAPTER V—PERSONAL RESPONSIBILITIES

Article 32. Relationship between Duties and Rights

1. Every person has responsibilities to his family, his community, and mankind.
2. The rights of each person are limited by the rights of others, by the security of all, and by the just demands of the general welfare, in a democratic society.

PART II—MEANS OF PROTECTION

CHAPTER VI—COMPETENT ORGANS

Article 33

The following organs shall have competence with respect to matters relating to the fulfillment of the commitments made by the States Parties to this Convention:

(*a*) the Inter-American Commission on Human Rights, referred to as "The Commission"; and

(*b*) The Inter-American Court of Human Rights, referred to as "The Court."

CHAPTER VII—INTER-AMERICAN COMMISSION ON HUMAN
RIGHTS

Section 1. Organization

Article 34

The Inter-American Commission on Human Rights shall be composed of seven members, who shall be persons of high moral character and recognized competence in the field of human rights.

Article 35

The Commission shall represent all the member countries of the Organization of American States.

Article 36

1. The members of the Commission shall be elected in a personal capacity by the General Assembly of the Organization from a list of candidates proposed by the governments of the member states.

2. Each of those governments may propose up to three candidates, who may be nationals of the states proposing them or of any other member state of the Organization of American States. When a slate of three is proposed, at least one of the candidates shall be a national of a state other than the one proposing the slate.

Article 37

1. The members of the Commission shall be elected for a term of four years and may be reelected only once, but the terms of three of the members chosen in the first election shall expire at the end of two years. Immediately following that election the General Assembly shall determine the names of those three members by lot.

2. No two nationals of the same state may be members of the Commission.

Article 38

Vacancies that may occur on the Commission for reasons other than the normal expiration of a term shall be filled by the Permanent Council of the Organization in accordance with the provisions of the Statute of the Commission.

Article 39

The Commission shall prepare its Statute, which it shall submit to the General Assembly for approval. It shall establish its own Regulations.

Article 40

Secretariat services for the Commission shall be furnished by the appropriate specialized unit of the General Secretariat of the Organization. This unit shall be provided with the resources required to accomplish the tasks assigned to it by the Commission.

Section 2. Functions

Article 41

The main function of the Commission shall be to promote respect for and defense of human rights. In the exercise of its mandate, it shall have the following functions and powers:

(*a*) to develop an awareness of human rights among the peoples of America;

(*b*) to make recommendations to the governments of the member states, when it considers such action advisable, for the adoption of progressive measures in favor of human rights within the framework of their domestic law and constitutional provisions as well as appropriate measures to further the observance of those rights;

(c) to prepare such studies or reports as it considers advisable in the performance of its duties;

(d) to request the governments of the member states to supply it with information on the measures adopted by them in matters of human rights;

(e) to respond, through the General Secretariat of the Organization of American States, to inquiries made by the member states on matters related to human rights and, within the limits of its possibilities, to provide those states with the advisory services they request;

(f) to take action on petitions and other communications pursuant to its authority under the provisions of Articles 44 through 51 of this Convention; and

(g) to submit an annual report to the General Assembly of the Organization of American States.

Article 42

The States Parties shall transmit to the Commission a copy of each of the reports and studies that they submit annually to the Executive Committees of the Inter-American Economic and Social Council and the Inter-American Council for Education, Science, and Culture, in their respective fields, so that the Commission may watch over the promotion of the rights implicit in the economic, social, educational, scientific, and cultural standards set forth in the Charter of the Organization of American States as amended by the Protocol of Buenos Aires.

Article 43

The States Parties undertake to provide the Commission with such information as it may request of them as to the manner in which their domestic law ensures the effective application of any provisions of this Convention.

Section 3. Competence

Article 44

Any person or group of persons, or any nongovernmental entity legally recognized in one or more member states of the Organization, may lodge petitions with the Commission containing denunciations or complaints of violation of this Convention by a State Party.

Article 45

1. Any State Party may, when it deposits its instrument of ratification of or adherence to this Convention, or at any later time, declare that it recognizes the competence of the Commission to receive and examine communications in which a State Party alleges that another State Party has committed a violation of a human right set forth in this Convention.

2. Communications presented by virtue of this article may be admitted and examined only if they are presented by a State Party that has made a declaration recognizing the aforementioned competence of the Commission. The Commission shall not admit any communication against a State Party that has not made such a declaration.

3. A declaration concerning recognition of competence may be made to be valid for an indefinite time, for a specified period, or for a specific case.

4. Declarations shall be deposited with the General Secretariat of the Organization of American States, which shall transmit copies thereof to the member states of that Organization.

Article 46

1. Admission by the Commission of a petition or communication lodged in accordance with Articles 44 or 45 shall be subject to the following requirements:

(*a*) that the remedies under domestic law have been pursued and exhausted in accordance with generally recognized principles of international law;

(*b*) that the petition or communication is lodged within a period of six months from the date on which the party alleging violation of his rights was notified of the final judgment;

(c) that the subject of the petition or communication is not pending in another international proceeding for settlement; and

(d) that, in the case of Article 44, the petition contains the name, nationality, profession, domicile, and signature of the person or persons or of the legal representative of the entity lodging the petition.

2. The provisions of paragraphs 1.a and 1.b of this article shall not be applicable when:

(a) the domestic legislation of the state concerned does not afford due process of law for the protection of the right or rights that have allegedly been violated;

(b) the party alleging violation of his rights has been denied access to the remedies under domestic law or has been prevented from exhausting them; or

(c) there has been unwarranted delay in rendering a final judgment under the aforementioned remedies.

Article 47

The Commission shall consider inadmissible any petition or communication submitted under Articles 44 or 45 if:

(a) any of the requirements indicated in Article 46 has not been met;

(b) the petition or communication does not state facts that tend to establish a violation of the rights guaranteed by this Convention;

(c) the statements of the petitioner or of the state indicate that the petition or communication is manifestly groundless or obviously out of order; or

(d) the petition or communication is substantially the same as one previously studied by the Commission or by another international organization.

Section 4. Procedure

Article 48

1. When the Commission receives a petition or communication alleging violation of any of the rights protected by this Convention, it shall proceed as follows:

(*a*) If it considers the petition or communication admissible, it shall request information from the government of the state indicated as being responsible for the alleged violations and shall furnish that government a transcript of the pertinent portions of the petition or communication. This information shall be submitted within a reasonable period to be determined by the Commission in accordance with the circumstances of each case.

(*b*) After the information has been received, or after the period established has elapsed and the information has not been received, the Commission shall ascertain whether the grounds for the petition or communication still exist. If they do not, the Commission shall order the record to be closed.

(*c*) The Commission may also declare the petition or communication inadmissible or out of order on the basis of information or evidence subsequently received.

(*d*) If the record has not been closed, the Commission shall, with the knowledge of the parties, examine the matter set forth in the petition or communication in order to verify the facts. If necessary and advisable, the Commission shall carry out an investigation, for the effective conduct of which it shall request, and the states concerned shall furnish to it, all necessary facilities.

(*e*) The Commission may request the states concerned to furnish any pertinent information and, if so requested, shall hear oral statements or receive written statements from the parties concerned.

(*f*) The Commission shall place itself at the disposal of the parties concerned with a view to reaching a friendly settlement of the matter on the basis of respect for the human rights recognized in this Convention.

2. However, in serious and urgent cases, only the presentation of a petition or communication that fulfills all the formal requirements of admissibility shall be necessary in order for the Commission to conduct an investigation with the prior consent of the state in whose territory a violation has allegedly been committed.

Article 49

If a friendly settlement has been reached in accordance with paragraph 1.f of Article 48, the Commission shall draw up a report, which shall be transmitted to the petitioner and to the States Parties to this Convention, and shall then be communicated to the Secretary General of the Organization of American States for publication. This report shall contain a brief statement of the facts and of the solution reached. If any party in the case so requests, the fullest possible information shall be provided to it.

Article 50

1. If a settlement is not reached, the Commission shall, within the time limit established by its Statute, draw up a report setting forth the facts and stating its conclusions. If the report, in whole or in part, does not represent the unanimous agreement of the members of the Commission, any member may attach to it a separate opinion. The written and oral statements made by the parties in accordance with paragraph 1.e of Article 48 shall also be attached to the report.

2. The report shall be transmitted to the states concerned, which shall not be at liberty to publish it.

3. In transmitting the report, the Committee may make such proposals and recommendations as it sees fit.

Article 51

1. If, within a period of three months from the date of the transmittal of the report of the Commission to the States concerned, the matter has not either been settled or submitted by the Commission or by the state concerned to the Court and its jurisdiction accepted, the Commission may, by the vote of an absolute majority of its members, set forth its opinion and conclusions concerning the question submitted for its consideration.

2. Where appropriate, the Commission shall make pertinent recommendations and shall prescribe a period within which the state is to take the measures that are incumbent upon it to remedy the situation examined.

3. When the prescribed period has expired, the Commis-

sion shall decide by the vote of an absolute majority of its members whether the state has taken adequate measures and whether to publish its report.

CHAPTER VIII—INTER-AMERICAN COURT OF HUMAN RIGHTS

Section 1. Organization

Article 52

1. The Court shall consist of seven judges, nationals of the member states of the Organization, elected in an individual capacity from among jurists of the highest moral authority and of recognized competence in the field of human rights, who possess the qualifications required for the exercise of the highest judicial functions in conformity with the law of the state of which they are nationals or of the state that proposes them as candidates.

2. No two judges may be nationals of the same state.

Article 53

1. The judges of the Court shall be elected by secret ballot by an absolute majority vote of the States Parties to the Convention, in the General Assembly of the Organization, from a panel of candidates proposed by those states.

2. Each of the States Parties may propose up to three candidates, nationals of the state that proposes them or of any other member state of the Organization of American States. When a slate of three is proposed, at least one of the candidates shall be a national of a state other than the one proposing the slate.

Article 54

1. The judges of the Court shall be elected for a term of six years and may be reelected only once. The term of three of the judges chosen in the first election shall expire at the end of three years. Immediately after the election, the names of the three judges shall be determined by lot in the General Assembly.

2. A judge elected to replace a judge whose term has not expired shall complete the term of the latter.

3. The judges shall continue in office until the expiration

of their term. However, they shall continue to serve with regard to cases that they have begun to hear and that are still pending, for which purposes they shall not be replaced by the newly elected judges.

Article 55

1. If a judge is a national of any of the States Parties to a case submitted to the Court, he shall retain his right to hear that case.

2. If one of the judges called upon to hear a case should be a national of one of the States Parties to the case, any other State Party in the case may appoint a person of its choice to serve on the Court as an *ad hoc* judge.

3. If among the judges called upon to hear a case none is a national of any of the States Parties to the case, each of the latter may appoint an *ad hoc* judge.

4. An *ad hoc* judge shall possess the qualifications indicated in Article 52.

5. If several States Parties to the Convention should have the same interest in a case, they shall be considered as a single party for purposes of the above provisions. In case of doubt, the Court shall decide.

Article 56

Five judges shall constitute a quorum for the transaction of business by the Court.

Article 57

The Commission shall appear in all cases before the Court.

Article 58

1. The Court shall have its seat at the place determined by the States Parties to the Convention in the General Assembly of the Organization; however, it may convene in the territory of any member state of the Organization of American States when a majority of the Court consider it desirable, and with the prior consent of the state concerned. The seat of the Court may be changed by the States Parties to the Convention in the General Assembly by a two-thirds vote.

2. The Court shall appoint its own secretary.

3. The Secretary shall have his office at the place where the Court has its seat and shall attend the meetings that the Court may hold away from its seat.

Article 59

The Court shall establish its Secretariat, which shall function under the direction of the Secretary of the Court, in accordance with the administrative standards of the General Secretariat of the Organization in all respect not incompatible with the independence of the Court. The staff of the Court's Secretariat shall be appointed by the Secretary General of the Organization, in consultation with the Secretary of the Court.

Article 60

The Court shall draw up its Statute which it shall submit to the General Assembly for approval. It shall adopt its own Rules of Procedure.

Section 2. Jurisdiction and Functions

Article 61

1. Only the States Parties and the Commission shall have the right to submit a case to the Court.

2. In order for the Court to hear a case, it is necessary that the procedures set forth in Articles 48 and 50 shall have been completed.

Article 62

1. A State Party may, upon depositing its instrument of ratification or adherence to this Convention, or at any subsequent time, declare that it recognizes as binding, *ipso facto*, and not requiring special agreement, the jurisdiction of the Court on all matters relating to the interpretation or application of this Convention.

2. Such declaration may be made unconditionally, on the condition of reciprocity, for a specified period, or for specific cases. It shall be presented to the Secretary General of the Organization, who shall transmit copies thereof to the other

member states of the Organization and to the Secretary of the Court.

3. The jurisdiction of the Court shall comprise all cases concerning the interpretation and application of the provisions of this Convention that are submitted to it, provided that the States Parties to the case recognize or have recognized such jurisdiction, whether by special declaration pursuant to the preceding paragraphs, or by a special agreement.

Article 63

1. If the Court finds that there has been a violation of a right or freedom protected by this Convention, the Court shall rule that the injured party be ensured the enjoyment of his right or freedom that was violated. It shall also rule, if appropriate, that the consequences of the measure or situation that constituted the breach of such right or freedom be remedied and that fair compensation be paid to the injured party.

2. In cases of extreme gravity and urgency, and when necessary to avoid irreparable damage to persons, the Court shall adopt such provisional measures as it deems pertinent in matters it has under consideration. With respect to a case not yet submitted to the Court, it may act at the request of the Commission.

Article 64

1. The member states of the Organization may consult the Court regarding the interpretation of this Convention or of other treaties concerning the protection of human rights in the American states. Within their spheres of competence, the organs listed in Chapter X of the Charter of the Organization of American States, as amended by the Protocol of Buenos Aires, may in like manner consult the Court.

2. The Court, at the request of a member state of the Organization, may provide that state with opinions regarding the compatibility of any of its domestic laws with the aforesaid international instruments.

Article 65

To each regular session of the General Assembly of the Organization of American States the Court shall submit, for the Assembly's consideration, a report on its work during the previous year. It shall specify, in particular, the cases in which a state has not complied with its judgments, making any pertinent recommendations.

Section 3. Procedure

Article 66

1. Reasons shall be given for the judgment of the Court.
2. If the judgment does not represent in whole or in part the unanimous opinion of the judges, any judge shall be entitled to have his dissenting or separate opinion attached to the judgment.

Article 67

The judgment of the Court shall be final and not subject to appeal. In case of disagreement as to the meaning or scope of the judgment, the Court shall interpret it at the request of any of the parties, provided the request is made within ninety days from the date of notification of the judgment.

Article 68

1. The States Parties to the Convention undertake to comply with the judgment of the Court in any case to which they are parties.
2. That part of a judgment that stipulates compensatory damages may be executed in the country concerned in accordance with domestic procedure governing the execution of judgments against the state.

Article 69

The parties to the case shall be notified of the judgment of the Court and it shall be transmitted to the States Parties to the Convention.

CHAPTER IX—COMMON PROVISIONS

Article 70

1. The judges of the Court and the members of the Commission shall enjoy, from the moment of their election and throughout their term of office, the immunities extended to diplomatic agents in accordance with international law. During the exercise of their official function they shall, in addition, enjoy the diplomatic privileges necessary for the performance of their duties.

2. At no time shall the judges of the Court or the members of the Commission be held liable for any decisions or opinions issued in the exercise of their functions.

Article 71

The position of judge of the Court or member of the Commission is incompatible with any other activity that might affect the independence or impartiality of such judge or member, as determined in the respective statutes.

Article 72

The judges of the Court and the members of the Commission shall receive emoluments and travel allowances in the form and under the conditions set forth in their statutes, with due regard for the importance and independence of their office. Such emoluments and travel allowances shall be determined in the budget of the Organization of American States, which shall also include the expenses of the Court and its Secretariat. To this end, the Court shall draw up its own budget and submit it for approval to the General Assembly through the General Secretariat. The latter may not introduce any changes in it.

Article 73

The General Assembly may only at the request of the Commission or the Court, as the case may be, determine sanctions to be applied against members of the Commission or judges of the Court when there are justifiable grounds for such action as set forth in the respective statutes. A vote of a two-thirds majority of the member states of the Organization shall be required for a decision in the case of members of the Commission and, in the case of judges of the Court, a two-thirds majority vote of the States Parties to the Convention shall also be required.

PART III—GENERAL AND TRANSITORY PROVISIONS

CHAPTER X—SIGNATURE, RATIFICATION, RESERVATIONS, AMENDMENTS, PROTOCOLS, AND DENUNCIATION

Article 74

1. This Convention shall be open for signature and ratification by or adherence of any member state of the Organization of American States.

2. Ratification of or adherence to this Convention shall be made by the deposit of an instrument of ratification or adherence with the General Secretariat of the Organization of American States. As soon as eleven states have deposited their instruments of ratification or adherence, the Convention shall enter into force. With respect to any state that ratifies or adheres thereafter, the Convention shall enter into force on the date of the deposit of its instrument of ratification or adherence.

3. The Secretary General shall inform all member states of the Organization of the entry into force of the Convention.

Article 75

This Convention shall be subject to reservations only in conformity with the provisions of the Vienna Convention on the Law of Treaties signed on May 23, 1969.

Article 76

1. Proposals to amend this Convention may be submitted to the General Assembly for the action it deems appropriate by any State Party directly, and by the Commission or the Court through the Secretary General.

2. Amendments shall enter into force for the states ratifying them on the date when two-thirds of the States Parties to this Convention have deposited their respective instruments of ratification. With respect to the other States Parties, the amendments shall enter into force on the dates on which they deposit their respective instruments of ratification.

Article 77

1. In accordance with Article 31, any State Party and the Commission may submit proposed protocols to this Convention for consideration by the States Parties at the General Assembly with a view to gradually including other rights and freedoms within its system of protection.

2. Each protocol shall determine the manner of its entry into force and shall be applied only among the States Parties to it.

Article 78

1. The States Parties may denounce this Convention at the expiration of a five-year period starting from the date of its entry into force and by means of notice given one year in advance. Notice of the denunciation shall be addressed to the Secretary General of the Organization, who shall inform the other States Parties.

2. Such a denunciation shall not have the effect of releasing the State Party concerned from the obligations contained in this Convention with respect to any act that may constitute a violation of those obligations and that has been taken by that state prior to the effective date of denunciation.

CHAPTER XI—TRANSITORY PROVISIONS

Section 1. Inter-American Commission on Human Rights

Article 79

Upon the entry into force of this Convention, the Secretary General shall, in writing, request each member state of the Organization to present, within ninety days, its candidates for membership on the Inter-American Commission on Human Rights. The Secretary General shall prepare a list in alphabetical order of the candidates presented, and transmit it to the member states of the Organization at least thirty days prior to the next session of the General Assembly.

Article 80

The members of the Commission shall be elected by secret ballot of the General Assembly from the list of candidates referred to in Article 79. The candidates who obtain the largest number of votes and an absolute majority of the votes of the representatives of the member states shall be declared elected. Should it become necessary to have several ballots in order to elect all the members of the Commission, the candidates who receive the smallest number of votes shall be eliminated successively, in the manner determined by the General Assembly.

Section 2. Inter-American Court of Human Rights

Article 81

Upon the entry into force of this Convention, the Secretary General shall, in writing, request each State Party to present, within ninety days, its candidates for membership on the Inter-American Court of Human Rights. The Secretary General shall prepare a list in alphabetical order of the candidtates presented and transmit it to the States Parties at least thirty days prior to the next session of the General Assembly.

Article 82

The judges of the Court shall be elected from the list of candidates referred to in Article 81, by secret ballot of the States Parties to the Convention in the General Assembly. The candidates who obtain the largest number of votes and an absolute majority of the votes of the representatives of the States Parties shall be declared elected. Should it become necessary to have several ballots in order to elect all the judges of the Court, the candidates who receive the smallest number of votes shall be eliminated successively, in the manner determined by the States Parties.

SELECTED BIBLIOGRAPHY

* * *

CONTRIBUTORS

*

SELECTED
BIBLIOGRAPHY

*   *   *

Editor's Note: The entries that follow are limited to publications appearing after the President's message of February 23, 1978.

Comment. *The International Human Rights Treaties: Some Problems of Policy and Interpretation.* 126 UNIVERSITY OF PENNSYLVANIA LAW REVIEW 886 (1978).

Goldklang, Jack M. *Letter to the Editors-in-Chief of the American Journal of International Law.* 74 AMERICAN JOURNAL OF INTERNATIONAL LAW 155 (1980).

Goldklang, Jack M. *Letter to the Editors of the Texas Law Review.* 57 TEXAS LAW REVIEW 859 (1979).

Henkin, Louis. *Rights: American and Human.* 79 COLUMBIA LAW REVIEW 405 (1979).

International Human Rights Treaties: Hearings before the Senate Committee on Foreign Relations, 96th Cong., 1st Sess. (1979).

Nanda, Ved P. *Human Rights and U.S. Foreign Policy Under Carter: Continuity and Change.* 8 DENVER JOURNAL OF INTERNATIONAL LAW AND POLICY 517 (1979).

Note. *The American Convention on Human Rights: The Propriety and Implications of United States Ratification.* 10 RUTGERS CAMDEN LAW JOURNAL 359 (1979).

Note. *The Covenant on Civil and Political Rights as the Law of the Land.* 25 VILLANOVA LAW REVIEW 119 (1979).

Note. *The Domestic Legal Effect of Declarations That Treaty Provisions Are Not Self-Executing.* 57 TEXAS LAW REVIEW 233 (1979).

Note. *International Covenant on Civil and Political Rights and United States Law: Department of State Proposals for Preserving the Status Quo.* 19 HARVARD INTERNATIONAL LAW JOURNAL 845 (1978).

Salzberg, John. *The Carter Administration: An Appraisal—A Congressional Perspective.* 8 DENVER JOURNAL OF INTERNATIONAL LAW AND POLICY 525 (1979).

Schachter, Oscar. *The Obligation of the Parties to Give Effect to the Covenant on Civil and Political Rights.* 73 AMERICAN JOURNAL OF INTERNATIONAL LAW 462 (1979).

Skelton, James W., Jr. *The United States Approach to Ratification of the International Covenants on Human Rights.* 1 HOUSTON JOURNAL OF INTERNATIONAL LAW 103 (1979).

Szasz, Paul C. *The International Legal Aspects of the Human Rights Program of the United States.* 12 CORNELL INTERNATIONAL LAW JOURNAL 161 (1979).

Weissbrodt, David. *United States Ratification of the Human Rights Covenants.* 63 MINNESOTA LAW REVIEW 35 (1978).

CONTRIBUTORS

*　　*　　*

Thomas Buergenthal is Dean and Professor of Law at the American University Law School.

Clyde Ferguson is Professor of Law at the Harvard Law School.

Jack Goldklang is an Attorney-Adviser in the Office of Legal Counsel of the U.S. Department of Justice.

Hurst Hannum is Executive Director of the Procedural Aspects of International Law Institute

Louis Henkin is University Professor at the Columbia Law School.

Richard B. Lillich is Howard W. Smith Professor of Law at the University of Virginia School of Law.

Nigel Rodley is Legal Adviser to Amnesty International, London.

Arthur Rovine is an Assistant Legal Adviser in the Office of the Legal Adviser of the U.S. Department of State.

Burns H. Weston is Professor of Law at the University of Iowa College of Law.